Wallace Bruce

The Hudson River and Routes from New York

To the White and Green mountains, Montreal, Lake George, Saratoga, Newport and Niagara

Falls

Wallace Bruce

The Hudson River and Routes from New York
To the White and Green mountains, Montreal, Lake George, Saratoga, Newport and Niagara Falls

ISBN/EAN: 9783743442191

Manufactured in Europe, USA, Canada, Australia, Japa

Cover: Foto ©Andreas Hilbeck / pixelio.de

Manufactured and distributed by brebook publishing software (www.brebook.com)

Wallace Bruce

The Hudson River and Routes from New York

The
Gordon Lester Ford
Collection
Presented by his Sons
Worthington Chauncey Ford
and
Paul Leicester Ford
to the
New York Public Library.

Bruce
FRM

TO THE
WHITE AND GREEN MOUNTAINS,
MONTREAL, LAKE GEORGE, SARATOGA,
NEWPORT and NIAGARA FALLS.

BY

THIRSTY McQUILL,

pseud. of Wallace Bruce.

For Sale at News Offices, and on Boats and Cars.

NEW YORK.
1872.

THE RECOLLET HOUSE,
MONTREAL.
BROWN & CLAGGETT,
IMPORTERS OF

Silks, Velvets, Shawls, Mantles, Real Laces and Ribbons.

One Thousand Dozen French Kid Gloves in all the new Shades and Styles.
Ladies and Gents Furnishings in Great Variety.
Ladies Costumes in Stock and made to order.

The Tweed and Cloth department is under the management of an able cutter. Gent garments got up on shortest notice and latest styles.
Strangers and Tourists should not fail to visit this Renowned Establishment, as they will always find a choice Stock of the latest Novelties.

Nos. 434, 436 & 438 Notre Dame Street, and Nos. 25, 27 & 29 St. Helen Street, West End,

R. G. BROWN.   MONTREAL.   C. C. CLAGGETT.

TOURIST GUIDE,

"To painted flowers, to trees upshooting hye,
To dales for shade, to hills for breathing space,
To river-view and lake with smiling face,
To trembling groves and crystal running bye."

"ENQUIRE WITHIN."

1872.

ESTABLISHED 1818.

SAVAGE, LYMAN & Co.,
271 NOTRE DAME ST., MONTREAL,

SOLE AGENTS FOR THE CELEBRATED

ULYSSE NARDIN WATCH.

THE FIRST PRIZE

Was Awarded the above Watch at the Annual Competition of the NATIONAL OBSERVATORY IN SWITZERLAND, for 1868 and 1869,

OVER ALL SWISS MANUFACTURERS.

ALSO IN STOCK,

WATCHES OF NOTED ENGLISH MAKERS.

THE LARGEST ASSORTMENT OF FINE JEWELRY IN THE DOMINION.

ELECTRO-PLATED WARE.

OPERA AND MARINE GLASSES.

LADIES' AND GENTS' DRESSING BAGS AND CASES FITTED COMPLETE.

FINE CUTLERY, MANTEL AND TRAVELING CLOCKS.

ALL KINDS OF JEWELRY MADE TO ORDER ON SHORT NOTICE.

CHAINS A SPECIALTY.

ALSO MANUFACTURERS OF SOLID SILVER WARE IN ALL ITS VARIETIES.

CAUTION.—Owing to the very great satisfaction given by the manufactures of ULYSSE NARDIN, many Watches are imported of the same name, spelt in different ways, and with other Christian names. There is but one **Ulysse Nardin**, of **Locle**, and his Watches and Chronometers can only be purchased from the Sole Agents, SAVAGE, LYMAN & CO., 271 Notre Dame Street, Sign of the Illuminated Clock.

P. S.—SAVAGE, LYMAN & Co., will remove during the coming season to those magnificent premises 226 & 228 St. James, corner of Dollard Street, sign of Illuminated Clock, a few doors east of the Ottawa Hotel.

FROM THE SEA

TO THE

NORTH WOODS.

A Condensed Sketch of the prominent points of interest on the Hudson, presenting at once an index to book, map and river.

Taking the Day Line of Steamers, the C. Vibbard and Daniel Drew (leaving Vestry street 8.30 A. M., 34th street 8.45,) you will see upon the West Bank of the river Hoboken and the Elysian Fields, Weehawken to the north of Elysian Fields, opposite 65th street.

Lunatic Asylum, on the right, between 115th and 120th streets, Manhattanville (Convent of the Sacred Heart), between 125th and 140th street.

Trinity Church Cemetery, above Manhattanville.

New York Institute for Deaf and Dumb, above Trinity Cemetery (a large building with cupola among the trees.)

Fort Washington, or Washington Heights, also on the right.

Fort Lee, on the left, almost opposite the Deaf and Dumb Institute. From this point the Palisades (300 to 500 feet high) reach about 12 miles to Rockland.

Spuyten Duyvel Creek (Harlem River), above Fort Washington, on the right, meets the Hudson. It reaches in South-easterly direction to East River, forming the Island of Manhattan or New York. (The Island is ten miles long, averaging about two miles in width.)

The Convent and Academy of Mt. St. Vincent, two miles above Spuyten Duyvel, originally built by Edwin Forrest for a residence.

Yonkers, two miles further, on the right.

Hastings, on the right, four miles north of Yonkers.

Dobb's Ferry, two miles above Hastings, (the river begins to widen into Tappan Bay)

Irvington, two miles above Dobb's Ferry, (23 from New York.)

Piermont, with its long pier, on the left.

Sunnyside, (formerly home of Washington Irving) half mile above Irvington, near the river bank, looking out from a shady grove.

Tarrytown, three miles above Irvington, (26 from New York.)

Sleepy Hollow, with its Burial Yard, one half mile above Tarrytown.

Nyack, opposite Tarrytown, (in the channel the ferry-boat connects with the Day Line.)

Sing Sing, six miles above Tarrytown, with its "marble halls," on the right.

Rockland Lake, on the left, between two hills (taken on faith). This is the source of the Hackensack River, and the great ice quarry for New York.

Croton River, on the right, above Sing Sing.

Croton Point, on the right, marks the northern part of Tappan Bay.

Haverstraw Bay, north of Croton Point. Here the river widens (almost four miles) into Haverstraw Bay. Haverstraw on the left; above this lime-stone quarries extend about half a mile.

Grassy Point, on the left, two miles above Haverstraw.

Stony Point, of Revolutionary fame, one mile further on the left.

Verplank's Point, on the right.

Peekskill, above Verplank's Point, on the right, 42 miles from New York.

Here the river bends suddenly to the west, Anthony's Nose on the right.

Fort Clinton and Fort Montgomery, on the left, under the shadow of the old Dunderberg. Iona Island, with its vineyards.

Buttermilk Falls, on the left.

Cozzens' Hotel, founded on a rock, on the left.

West Point, one mile above, on the left.

Garrison, directly opposite (Highland House on a fine plateau, about half a mile from the river).

Kosciusko's monument on the left.

Fort Putnam looking down upon it.

Turning the Point, we see Roe's Hotel.

Cold Spring, on the right, 53 miles from New York.

Old Crow Nest, opposite Cold Spring.

Undercliff, (former home of Morris,) on the right.

(VIEW ON THE HUDSON.)
Soldiers Memorial Fountain, Poughkeepsie.

Break Neck, on the right. Storm King, on the left.
Cornwall, just above Storm King.
Idlewild, (former home of Willis,) about one mile north of Cornwall on the road to Newburh.
Newburgh Bay opens here to the north of the Highlands.
Washington's Headquarters, on the southern declivity of Newburgh.
Fishkill Landing, opposite Newburgh, on the right.
New Hamburgh, on the right, at the mouth of Wappinger Creek, 65 miles from New York.
Poughkeepsie, on the right, 73 miles from New York.
Hyde Park, six miles to the north, connected with Poughkeepsie by a succession of villas ; the finest drive on the river.
Rhinecliff, on the right, 88 miles from New York.
Rhinebeck, two miles from Rhinecliff (back from the river).
Rondout, opposite. Here persons take the cars for "Overlook Mountain House."
Tivoli, on the right, 98 miles from New York.
Saugerties, opposite, on the left.
Germantown, on the right, 104 miles from New York.
Man in the Mountain. Between Germantown and Catskill we get the finest view of the Man in the Mountain.
Catskill, on the left, 111 miles from New York. Here stages connect with Catskill Mountain House. Prospect Park Hotel directly above the landing, on the left.
Hudson, on the right, 115 miles from New York. Here passengers take the cars for Lebanon Springs. Athens, across the river from Hudson.
Stockport, on the right. Coxsackie, on the left.
Stuyvesant, on the right, 124 miles from New York.
New Baltimore and Coeymans, on the left.
Schodack and Castleton, on the right.
Albany, on the left, 142 miles from New York.
Greenbush, on the right.
Troy, six miles north of Greenbush.
West Troy, on the left, six miles north of Albany. Persons *en*

route for Niagara Falls take Central Railroad at Albany ; for Saratoga and Lake George, take Rensselaer and Saratoga Railroad, either at Albany or Troy.

At Troy, the Rensselaer and Saratoga Railroad crosses the Hudson and passes up the west bank as far as Mechanicsville; the railroad then takes a westerly course to Ballston Spa, then to the north-east to Saratoga Springs. At Fort Edward the railroad again crosses the river and passes through Dunham's Basin, Smith's Basin, Fort Ann, and Comstock's Landing to Whitehall; thence passengers can go to Rutland and the north by rail, or to Burlington and Plattsburgh by the Champlain boats.

Returning to Fort Edward, you will see by the map that the river forms almost a half circle around Sandy Hill and Glen's Falls, but at Luzerne (where the Sacandaga meets it) again finds its general southerly course. It seems to pass around Lake George, as if the Hudson, even in its infancy, instinctively turned aside from rival beauty. Above Stony Creek the Schroon River brings the waters of Schroon Lake to the Hudson, and the left branch of the Hudson takes us to the Lakes of Essex County, about four thousand feet above the sea, under the shadows of Mount Seward, Mount Marcy, and McAntyre.

Thus, in brief, we have traced the Hudson—as it were, through four phases—and we venture a poetical division, viz: The dreamy repose of the Palisades and Tappan Zee ; the magnificent grandeur and sublimity of the Highlands ; the ever-changing beauty of the Catskills, and the wildness of the Adirondacks. No other river in the world is ever compared with the Hudson except the Rhine. The latter has, it is true, castled towers and vineyards, and poetic traditions of a thousand years; but face to face with Nature, the Hudson has no rival. The Rhine flows 600 miles through a low, flat country, before you reach its interest. And no tourist ever thinks of starting at the sea; he takes 600 miles of railroad to reach a respectable starting point. The interest of the Hudson commences at the very portal of our country; and if Cicero could flatter himself by saying, "Oh, Rome! fortunate in having such a consul!" we can be excused in saying, New York is happy in having at its very doors such a river.

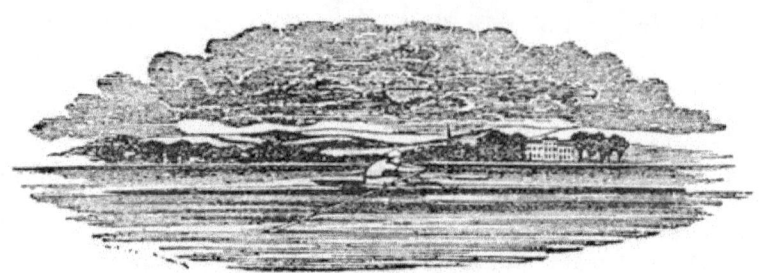

PAPER BOATS

HAVE BEEN ROWED BY THE WINNERS OF
ONE HUNDRED AND FIFTY MATCHED RACES
SINCE THEIR INTRODUCTION IN 1868.

For racing and training they are prefered to those of wood by the midshipmen at the United States Naval Academy, by numerous Boat Clubs, and by numbers of the best Oarsmen in the country.

NOW READY:
The Illustrated Catalogue and Oarsman's Manual.

One large Quarto Volume, 500 pages, printed in colors, on tinted paper, containing 65 fine Illustrations on wood, and twelve plates on stone, (four 12 x 40 inches,) bound in gilt muslin, bevelled edges, SOLD AT COST, price $6.50. Sent to any part of the country on receipt of price.

BOATS
FOR

Racing, Hunting, Traveling, Exercise, or Pleasure, made of Paper,

ARE BUILT ONLY BY

WATERS, BALCH & CO.,
SOLE MANUFACTURERS AND PATENTEES,

259 RIVER STREET, TROY, N. Y.

Enclose Stamp for Circulars.

THE HUDSON.

The Hudson has been called the Shate-muck, the Mohegan, the Manhattan, the Noordt Montaigne, the Mauritius, the North River, and the River of the Mountains. It was called the Hudson River, not by the Dutch as generally stated, but by the English, as Henry Hudson was an Englishman, although he sailed from a Dutch port, with a Dutch crew, and a Dutch vessel. The river was called the Mauritius in a letter to

OLOFFE VAN KORTLANDT'S DREAM.

the "High and mighty Lords" of Holland, written November 5, 1626. It was called the North River to distinguish it from the Delaware, called the South River. The Spaniards called it the River of the Mountains. It was discovered in the year 1609. The town of Communipaw was founded soon after, and according to Knickerbocker,—whose quiet humor is always read and re-read with pleasure,—might justly be considered the mother colony of our glorious city: for lo! the sage Oloffe Van

Kortlandt dreamed a dream, and the good St. Nicholas came riding over the tops of the trees and descended upon the island of Manhattan and sat himself down and smoked, "and the smoke ascended into the sky, and formed a cloud over head, and Oloffe bethought him and he hastened and climbed up to the top of one of the tallest trees and saw that the smoke spread over a great extent of country; and as he considered it more attentively he fancied that the great volume assumed a variety of marvelous forms, where, in dim obscurity, he saw shadowed out palaces and domes and lofty spires, all of which lasted but a moment, and then passed away." So our city, like Alba Longa and Rome, and other cities of antiquity, was under the immediate care of its tutelar saint. Its destiny was foreshadowed, for now the palaces and domes and lofty spires are real and genuine, and something more than dreams are made of.

At Weehawken, where the duel took place between Hamilton and Burr, 1804, about three miles north of Hoboken, it is said the Indians first became intoxicated, and from the difficulty they experienced in keeping a straight line, they conceived the idea that the Hudson must in some period of the world's history have become *inebriated*, to have made such a winding channel to the sea; and they imagined that somewhere in the northern forests, near some favorite haunt of the Great Spirit, a fountain of this "fire water," clear and sparkling, bubbled from the ground, and the river, drinking this water as it flowed into its bosom, naturally formed a wandering way to the sea. In accordance with this theory, they rejected their former idea, that the Highlands had ever been sundered, and chose rather to believe that the mountains and little hills, impelled by curiosity, had come from the East and the West to see this strange phenomenon, and either attracted by each other's beauty, or loving the music of the water, had willingly remained upon its banks. To find this wonderful fountain, the warriors were willing to encounter any perils and endure any hardships. Every little lake in the North Woods which found an outlet in the river was visited with a zeal and eagerness which gives the blush to modern explorers; every trickling rivulet was tasted, but the clear, cold water only laughed merrily in their faces and sweetly kissed their parched lips as they stooped to drink of its purity. Up the tributary

MOUNT DORSET, NORTH OF THE PLEASANT VILLAGE OF MANCHESTER, VERMONT, OVERLOOKING THE SOURCE OF THE BATTENKILL.

Under this mountain rises the Battenkill, one of the northern tributaries of the Hudson, where the Indians searched (in vain) for the "Fire Water Fountain."

N. B.—The Hudson has, therefore, *Yankee blood* in her veins, *direct* from the *Green Mountains*.

streams, far into the land of the Mohawks, almost to the hunting grounds of the Oneidas; up the rapid Sacandaga to beautiful "Lake Pleasant," mirroring in its sleeping waters the same pines and hemlocks as two hundred years ago; along the bright-flowing Hoosic, beyond the "Strange Chimney" of doubtful utility, and the ever-green "Council Square," where the tribes were wont to assemble in the realm of the Schacokes; up the Battenkill to the clear fountain which murmurs a response to the gentle flowing of Otter Creek, on its way to the blue waters of Champlain; up the Poestenkill, honored in later years by an improbable legend; up the Kinderhook and Claverack creeks, frequently referred to in rythmic measure by the fair daughters of Columbia; far away to the Taghconic range, whose eastern slope loses its waters in the deep ravines of the old Stockbridge chiefs, and the beautiful hills where the Green River and Jansen's Creek, born of twin fountains, bid each other an early adieu; the former seeking the valley of the Housatonic, while the latter, joyful with the music of Bash-Bish, brings to the eastern bank of the river a heart full of traditional beauty. But in vain! The Helderberg Hills and the lordly Catskills gave no token of this strange fountain, more wonderful than those fountains of love and hatred near the fabled palace of Alcina. The warriors only returned to speak of the crystal lakes and little brooklets, whose sources, deeply buried in the northern forests for long years, will never know the sunshine.

But we must not overlook the fact that it is moreover stated by tradition, the *gravest* of all historians, that during this search they discovered the "Springs," and on their return attempted to describe to their astonished brethren, with distorted visages which resembled rubber countenances considerably squeezed, the taste of these health-giving mineral waters, which society long ago countenanced, and in many cases still *countenances* in a manner very like the original discoverers. On the east side of the river between 73d and 74th streets is the Orphan Asylum, and five miles from 30th street we come to Manhattanville, where the Bloomingdale road loses its pretty name and is again called Broadway. The chief attractions are the Catholic Schools—the Convent of the Sacred Heart for girls, and Manhattan College for boys. Passing 152d

(VIEW ON THE HUDSON.)
Marble Enclosure of the Eastman Grounds, Poughkeepsie.

Street and Fort Washington, we come to Spuyten Duyvel Creek, to the north of Washington Heights. It is said the creek derived its name from the following *incident*. Peter Stuyvesant, the governor of New Amsterdam, sent his trumpeter, Antony von Corlear, on an important message up the river:

"It was a dark and stormy night when the good Antony arrived at the famous creek (sagely denominated Harlaem River) which separates the island of Manhattan from the mainland. The wind was high, the elements were in an uproar, and no Charon could be found to ferry the adventurous sounder of brass across the water. For a short time he vapored like an impatient ghost upon the brink, and then, bethinking himself of the urgency of his errand, took a hearty embrace of his stone bottle, swore most valorously that he would swim across *en spijt en Duyrel* (in spite of the Devil!) and daringly plunged into the stream. Luckless Antony! Scarce had he buffeted half way over when he was observed to struggle violently, as if battling with the spirit of the waters; instinctively he put his trumpet to his mouth, and giving a vehement blast, sank forever to the bottom."

About two miles above this creek, where it is said Henry Hudson had a little "unpleasantness" with the Indians, October 22, 1608, we see on the right bank the former residence of Mr. Forrest, a castle structure, which soon after the famous divorce suit he sold to the Catholic Sisters of Charity belonging to the Convent and Academy of Mt. St. Vincent. About two miles to the north is the town of Yonkers, so named from the "young heir" or "young sir" of the Phillipsie manor. This was the birthplace of Mary Phillipsie, of whom Washington became enamored in 1759. The old manor house is still standing, purchased a short time ago by the village of Yonkers, and converted for the most part into offices for transacting town affairs. The older portion of the house was built in 1682; the present front in 1745. The wood-work is very interesting, and the ceilings, the large hall, and wide fireplace. In the room pointed out as Washington's room, the fireplace still retains the old tiles, "illustrating familiar passages in Bible history," fifty on each side, looking as clear as if they were made but yesterday. The Getty House is a fine hotel, one of the best in Westchester County. Here is also a fine school conducted by Benjamin Mason, known as the "Yonkers Military Institute." Here the sports are made an important auxiliary to a boy's education, and the place possesses unsurpassed facilities for Skating, Boating, and Swimming. Passing through Glenwood and Hastings we come to Dobbs' Ferry, five miles from Yonkers, the scene of a marvelous legend. We would hardly dare vouch for its truthfulness, and the nearer we get to the locality we are sorry to say the less it is believed, and yet the account was told us in our childhood for very truth.

THE MYTHICAL CASTLE OF DOBBS' FERRY.

The Legend of Dobbs' Ferry;
OR,
THE MARITAL FATE OF HENDRICK AND KATRINA.

On the banks of the Hudson near old Dobbs' Ferry,
A castle once stood deserted and dreary,
Around whose towers the ivy crept,
Around whose walls even silence slept.
Silent and sad was the ruined place,
As it were the grave of a buried race.
Tradition says that long ago—
Perhaps two hundred years or so—

A family came from a town somewhere,
With obvious intentions of settling there;
For this castle they built prodigious in size,
Which filled the neighbors with such surprise
That it literally made them stick out their eyes.
And as the right is with the strong,
No way had they to redress the wrong;
But, strange to say, on a certain day,
A woman in white on the grounds appeared,
Perhaps a fairy, perhaps a fay,
And marshaled them all and led them away,
For all who looked upon her feared,
And trembling could not but obey.
And so, deserted were those halls,
For none returned who once were seen,
And very few were those I ween
Who dared to pass those castle walls;
And many the legends mysterious and queer,
About that home of perpetual fear.
'T was said that often at midnight hour,
When the moon was full on the castle tower,
Her cold light trembled with fitful glare,
And music strange filled earth and air,
As 't were a dirge for the freed from pain,
Or sorrow subdued for those that remain—
Sorrow! of all life's song the refrain!

    Stranger than all the other stories
    Was the story of a wedding,
    Or the fate of Mr. Hendrick
    And his darling, Miss Katrina.
    It was up among the Highlands,
    And the "You do" and the "I will"
    Just had made the two a unit,
    When in white there came a fairy,
    Took the hand of Miss Katrina,
    And they vanished in a minute.
    Oh! the sorrow and the wailing!
    They were gone, and none knew whither.
    Hendrick's heart was almost broken;
    Where's Katrina? Where's Katrina?
    After many days of mourning
    It was said that near the castle,
    Near the ruin of Dobbs' Ferry—
    Ruin now that's quite forgotten,
    Two were seen both dressed as fairies.

Night and day about the castle.
Hendrick wept and prayed and listened,
But he only heard the echo,
Heard the echo of his wailing.
Filled with grief and disappointment,
On the seventh night, in the twilight,
He begins to hum this measure,
And his heart was almost breaking:—

It is sweet to sit at evening, when the west is painted red,
And to think of friends once with us, of the living and the dead;
It is sweet to hear at midnight, music stealing through the air,
While we feel our spirits rising heavenward on that silver stair.
Ever fonder, ever dearer, seems our youth that hastened by,
And we love to live in memory when our fond hopes fade and die;
Yes, like forests that seem fairer when the leaves their freshness lose,
So the past, those leaves now fading, tinged with memory lovelier grows.

The echoes startled from their sleep
Had hardly died away,
When forth from out the shadows deep
The fairy held her way;
No shadow she threw in the moon's pale beams,
But, like a passing form of light,
Presented herself to our hero's sight,
Quite lost in sorrow and his dreams.
And thus the fairy began to say:—
I 've watched you, Hendrick, for many a day,
Weeping and wailing, but all in vain,
For ne'er can you see your darling again.
Weep for Katrina with eyes so blue;
Weep! well you may, for she was true.
Few maidens ever loved as she;
Weep! weep! it does n't trouble me:
But though I am not moved by pity,
I admire you for your courage,
And, if you can guess a riddle,
I will make you, too, immortal,
So that you can live forever
With your darling, your Katrina.

Where grows the flower, and what 's its name,
Which blooms in winter and summer the same,
The language of which some say is true,
Some say is false; now what say you?

Our hero knew not what to say
In answer to the cruel fay;
But a muse, from a bright and distant sphere,
Swiftly to his rescue flew,
And, breathing softly in his ear,
Whispered the *answer* plain and clear;
And to the fairy, mute with surprise,
He answered somewhat in this wise:—

Say not all the flowers of the valley fade,
When painted leaves on the ground are laid,
And the carpet of nature, curiously dyed,
Covers the vale and the mountain side;
Oh! no; there's a flower *earth's frost* never nips
In many a valley—the sweet *two-lips*.

We find them in bowers of nature wild
Wherever we see the forest child,
Where'er streamlets flow or soft winds blow,
In lands that are wrapped in eternal snow,
We find these flowers; for sun or shade
Ne'er blights or blasts or makes them fade;
And even more than this is true,
For when *they're pressed* they bloom anew.

The fairy vanished but again appeared
Leading Katrina through the ruined halls,
And in the silence of that midnight hour,
Again were joined those hands once rudely torn.
We leave the hearer here to guess the rest,
How many times "two-lips" were fondly pressed;
How long they sat and watched the moonlight fall
Upon the ruined tower and ivied wall.
And still some people of that section say,
That when the stars roll in their middle way,
The immortal pair amid the ruins stand,
Just as they should be, *always hand in hand*.

A little north of Dobbs' Ferry is Irvington, and about half a mile above the depot, and near the railroad, is "Sunny Side," once known as "Wolfert Roost," but transformed into beauty, like every thing which the hand of Irving touched. Two miles to the north is

TARRYTOWN.

with its old Dutch church, its Sleepy Hollow, and quiet burial-yard,

(VIEW ON THE HUDSON.)
Fairy Land Realized.

where Irving lies buried. A plain slab with this inscription marks his resting-place:—

WASHINGTON IRVING.
Born, April 3d, 1783,
Died, November 28th, 1859.

Tarrytown and vicinity possess much of historic interest, and a summer week could be delightfully passed here at the Franklin House. This was the very heart of the debatable ground of the Revolution, and here, according to Irving, arose the two great orders of border chivalry—the Skinners and the Cow Boys. The former fought or rather marauded under the American, the latter under the British banner. "In the zeal of service both were apt to make blunders, and confounded the property of friend and foe. Neither of them in the heat and hurry of a foray had time to ascertain the politics of a horse or cow which they were driving off into captivity, nor when they wrung the neck of a rooster did they trouble their heads whether he crowed for Congress or King George." According to Lossing, the Indians called Tarrytown "A-lip Conck," or place of elms; the Dutch called it Terwen Dorp or Wheat town, hence Tarrytown; but Knickerbocker's natural philosophy believed that it arose from the tarrying of husbands at the village tavern. Here, on the old post road, Major André was captured and a monument erected on the spot by the people of Westchester County, Oct. 7, 1853, with this inscription:—

ON THIS SPOT
THE 23D DAY OF SEPTEMBER, 1780, THE SPY
MAJOR JOHN ANDRE,
Adjutant-General of the British Army, was captured by
JOHN PAULDING, DAVID WILLIAMS, AND ISAAC VAN WART,
ALL NATIVES OF THIS COUNTY.
History has told the rest.

In a pleasant part of the village is the "Irving Institute," established in 1838: situated about half a mile from the depot, it commands charming views of the Hudson and of the inland scenery. D. S. Rowe is Principal, who has had long experience and success as a teacher. We present a fine out of his buildings and grounds. Opposite Tarrytown is Nyack. At this point of the river the Tappan Zee is about three miles wide, and as we look out upon its tranquil waters it does not seem as if it were haunted either by "the old Storm Ship," which went up the Hudson and never returned, or by the Flying Dutchman who still rows but never makes a port. It is said by the old inhabitants, but only the credulous believe it, that often in the still twilight of summer evening, when the sea

THE IRVING INSTITUTE.

is like glass and the opposite hills throw their shadows across it, that the low, vigorous pull of oars is heard, but no boat is seen. It seems that a certain Mr. "Van Dam," of graceless memory, attended a quilting frolic at Kakiat, on the opposite shore, one Saturday afternoon; having imbibed rather freely, and danced until midnight, he thought it high time to return. He was warned of the Sabbath's approach, and the verge of Sunday morning, but like Tam O'Shanter, he pulled off—

"That hour of night's black arch the key-stone,"

swearing he would not land until he reached Spuyten Duyvel if it took him a month of Sundays. "He was never seen afterward, but may still be heard plying his oars, being the Flying Dutchman of the Tappan Zee, doomed to ply between Kakiat and Spuyten Duyvel until the day of judgment."

Smith's Ferry connects Tarrytown and Nyack. Here is a fine hotel, the St. Nicholas, J. A. Demarest, proprietor, one of the finest conducted between New York and Albany. South of Nyack is Piermont, the pier is about one mile in length; this was formerly the terminus of the Erie railroad; about three miles west from the river, is the old village of Tappan, the name of Indian origin. Here André was hung, and buried near the "Stone House of 76." In 1821 his bones were removed to Westminster Abbey. To the north of Nyack is Rockland, whose lake on the hill, one hundred and sixty feet above the river, furnishes ice for New York. This is the source of the Hackensack River. A little to the north of Rockland is Haverstraw, where Arnold and André met for the first time.

Returning to the east bank of the river we pass through Scarborough, four miles north of Tarrytown, and one mile beyond is Sing Sing. The walls of the prison are close to the river, perhaps suggesting to poetical natures, "Loch Leman lies by Chillon's walls." About two miles north of Sing Sing is Croton or Teller's Point, near this is the mouth of Croton, River. About six miles from its mouth there is a dam across the Croton forming a lake five miles long. This lake furnishes New York with water. An aqueduct carries it over thirty miles, crossing the Harlem River, via High Bridge, built of granite, fourteen hundred and fifty feet long, and over one hundred feet high. We will see the Croton again among the hills and valleys of Carmel and Lake Mahopac, in our sketch of the Harlem Valley. Passing through Crugers we come to Verplanck's Point, and almost opposite Stony Point, where at two o'clock one morning Wayne penned the brief dispatch to Washington, "The American flag waves here." The river between these points is only about half a mile wide. Passing through Montrose we come to

PEEKSKILL,

where Nathan Palmer the spy was hung, and another brief letter, *with a postscript penned* by Israel Putnam. Here is the Continental Hotel, a pleasant house kept by Mr. Sutten, its pleasant verandas reminding one of the days of which the historian of New York loved to write. This was the birthplace of Paulding, who died here in 1818. There is a monument to his memory about two miles north of the village. Above Peekskill is Anthony's Nose, elevated twelve hundred and twenty-eight feet, and it might well be called a prominent *feature* of the Hudson. Its name according to Irving is derived from the nose of Anthony Van Corlear, the illustrious trumpeter of Peter Stuyvesant. "Now thus it happened that bright and early in the morning the good Anthony, having washed his burly visage, was leaning over the quarter railing of the galley, contemplating it in the glassy waves below. Just at this moment the illustrious sun breaking in all its splendor from behind a high bluff of the Highlands did dart one of his most potent beams full upon the refulgent *nose* of the sounder of brass, the reflection of which shot straight way down hissing hot into the water, and killed a mighty sturgeon that was sporting beside the vessel. When this astonishing miracle was made known to the governor, and he tasted of the unknown fish, he marveled exceedingly, and as a monument thereof he gave the name of Anthony's Nose to a stout promontory in the neighborhood, and it has continued to be called Anthony's Nose ever since." On the west side of the river is the famous Dunderberg Mountain. From Anthony's Nose to Fort Montgomery a chain was extended in the time of the Revolution, and some of the links are in the Albany State Library. Just above Anthony's Nose is Sugar Loaf Mountain, at the foot of which is Beverly Dock, where Arnold escaped to the *Vulture*. On the west side a little to the north is Buttermilk Falls, and Cozzen's Hotel stands out bold and commanding from an elevation of about two hundred feet. About a mile to the north of Cozzen's Hotel we see the military school of

WEST POINT.

The plateau is about two hundred feet above the river. The land, about two hundred and fifty acres, was ceded to the United States by New York in 1826. The Hudson is here less than half a mile in width. Near the northern extremity of the ground is the monument of Kosciusko with the inscription

KOSCIUSKO.
Erected by the Corps of Cadets, 1828.

Near the river is a niche in the cliff called Kosciusko's Garden, and the indenture of a cannon-ball is pointed out which must have disturbed the patriot's meditations. Five hundred and ninety-six feet above the river are the ruins of Fort Putnam. Turning the point we obtain a fine view of Roe's Hotel. A bronze statute of General John Sedgwick was erected two years ago on the parade ground. It is something of a coincidence that he should lie buried in Cornwall, Connecticut, and a statue and tablet to his memory stand in the town of Cornwall, New York.

GARRISON.

Opposite West Point is the station Garrison, on the Hudson River Railroad; and about a half mile from the depot is the "Highland House," standing on a magnificent plateau. We call attention to the fact that this is *not* the Highland House near Cozzen's, neither is it the little house at the ferry crossing, as unpleasant mistakes have sometimes been made, but "The Highland House," about four hundred feet above the river, appropriately named, lying in the very center of the Highlands. Its proprietors are descendants of the family who lived here in the time of the Revolution, from whom the ferry and landing took their name. The house has been recently enlarged to almost double its former capacity. Its location is certainly one of the finest along the river. The plateau is inclosed by the North Redoubt and South Redoubt Mountains, reaching from Sugar Loaf and Anthony's Nose, on the south, to Breakneck on the north. The ruins of the redoubt are often visited, and many points of our early history lying in the immediate vicinity. South of us are the Arnold House and Beverly Dock, where Arnold fled from the curses of his people, here Washington, Putnam and old Mad Anthony struggled for the good cause, here beyond a question the wife of Putnam was buried, and here are local legends—those unclaimed children of history—waiting for their relationship to be acknowledged. Surely there is no place where the history of our country can be studied with greater interest than among these wild fastnesses where freedom found protection.

HIGHLAND HOUSE, GARRISON, NEW YORK.
G. F. & W. D. GARRISON, PROPRIETORS AND OWNERS.

Wander where you will, the surrounding mountains abound with wild and picturesque glens. Poet, artist, novelist, and historian, *all* who find books in running brooks, continually add their testimony to the accumulating evidence. In brief, all who wish to spend a summer pleasantly and profitably will find the "Highland House,"—a cut of which is here given—one of the finest family hotels on the Hudson River. Its location is picturesque and healthy, on higher ground than West Point, and commanding a full view. The scenery and drives of the Highlands are very fine. There is one incident connected with the Traitor of American History which we think will be interesting as a lesson of remorse. He escaped to the *Vulture* on the morning of September 24, 1780. Arnold was at this time in command of West Point. Three days before he met André to complete the sale of his country. The morning of the 24th, Alexander Hamilton and General La Fayette were at Arnold's house. All three were seated at breakfast, and while eating, a letter was handed to Arnold from Jamison. He read its contents and excused himself from the table, went to his room, bade his wife good-bye, kissed his little boy in the cradle, and fleeing from the curses of a whole people, took refuge in the *Vulture*. It is said that one day when Talleyrand arrived in Havre on foot from Paris, in the darkest hour of the French Revolution, pursued by the bloodhounds of the reign of terror, he was about to secure a passage to the United States, and asked the landlord of the hotel : " So there are Americans staying at your house? I am going across the water, and would like a letter to a person of influence in the New World." " There is a gentleman up-stairs from Britain or America," was the response. He pointed the way and Talleyrand ascended the stairs. In a dimly lighted room sat the man of whom the great minister of France was to ask a favor. He advanced and poured forth in elegant French and broken English: "I am a wanderer and an exile. I am forced to fly to the New World without a friend or home. You are an American. Give me, then, I beseech you, a letter of yours, so that I may be able to earn my bread." The strange gentleman rose. With a look that Talleyrand never forgot, he retreated toward the door of the next chamber. He spoke as he retreated, and his voice was full of suffering: "I am the only man of the New World who can raise his hand to God and say, 'I have not a friend, not one, in America.'" " Who are you?" he cried. "Your name?" "My name is Benedict Arnold." Would that our modern traitors had the same vulture at their vitals as in the early days of the Republic, when treason was made odious without the aid of politicians.

About three miles to the north is "Undercliff," where Morris put the beauties of the Hudson into the sweetest verse ; and about eleven or twelve at night, in the months of July or August, the passenger of the New York and northern boats who appreciates the sublimity of these mountains more than an hour of sleep, will see a lone star above the mountains; and in the midst of the gloom, and the toiling of the machinery, and the heaving of the waters as they dash against the banks that are here narrowed into beauty, he will feel, when opposite "Undercliff," the full force and beauty of the lines,

> "Old Cro-nest like a monarch stands,
> Crowned with a single star."

And also the musical lines of Rodman Drake,

> "'Tis the middle watch of a summer night,
> The earth is dark, but the heavens are bright,
> The moon looks down on old Cro-nest,
> She mellows the shade on his shaggy breast,
> And seems his huge gray form to throw,
> In a silver cone, on the wave below."

We have now come through twenty miles of scenery unequaled in the world, when we consider the points of history, poetry, and beauty, all blended together. The river seems like a succession of beautiful lakes, "shut in by towering hills from the rude world." "The rocks, the rills, the woods, and templed hills" are full of history and poetry; and we imagine that not even the castled Rhine is more beautiful than the Hudson. In the lines of Hoffman,

> "What though no cloister gray or ivied column
> Along this cliff their somber ruins rear;
> What though no frowning tower or temple solemn
> Of despots tell and superstition here,
> Yet sights and sounds at which the world have wondered,
> Within these wild ravines have had their birth;
> Young freedom's cannon from these glens have thundered,
> And sent their startling echoes o'er the earth;
> And not a verdant glade or mountain hoary
> But treasures up within the glorious story."

Above Cold Spring is Bull Hill, or in our classical times called Mount Taurus, 1,586 feet in height, and Breakneck Hill, where the tourist once looked for "Turk's Face." A part of it was blasted away for a fortification in Mexico. It almost spoiled his photograph. Beacon Hill, 1,685 feet high, is the last of the Highlands on the eastern bank of the river. On the western side, Butter Hill, or, according to the christening of Willis, Storm Cliff, 1,529 feet high. These mark the northern pass of the Highlands. The Highlands are a part of the Alleghanian chain of mountains. To the east they reach away under the name of the Fishkill Mountains, until they strike the Taconic, or Taghkannic Mountains. The range is about twenty miles in width where it crosses the Hudson. Northwest of the Highlands are the Shawungunk Mountains, followed by the Catskills, which to the north of Hudson trend off to the northwest, and are known as the Helderberg Hills. The highest summit of the chain is said to be Round Top, in Greene County, 3,804 feet in altitude. Storm King is the most abrupt of the Highlands. It is literally a mountain rock, with sides scarred and torn by storms and lightning. To the north lies the pleasant little village of Cornwall, a great resort for summer boarders. About a mile to the north of the village, on the old road to Newburgh, is "Idlewild," once the home of Willis. Near this point we obtain a fine view of the beautiful bay of Newburgh. From the river boats we get a fine view of the terraced city,

NEWBURGH.

Newburgh was settled by the Palatines, in the year 1708. The United States Hotel near the landing, recently purchased, by the Goodsell Brothers, from Cozzens, West Point, is the best hotel, and there is also a summer resort connected with it, a short distance from the city. To the south of the city, is the old Stone House, "Washington's Head-Quarters." Here we see many relics of the Revolution; old Hessian boots that were never intended for flight, making either victory, or capture inevitable; old swords that have a history written in blood; trappings of soldiers that have lost the glitter and the tinsel, "the pride, the pomp and circumstance of glorious war;" and a piano, of most harmonious discord. The afternoon that we had the pleasure of visiting this collection of antiquity, we found an enthusiastic individual from Boston playing "The Sword of Bunker Hill." We never heard any thing in prose, poetry, or music exactly like it, but it suggested,

"The graves stood tenantless, and the sheeted dead
Did *squeak* and *gibber* in the very streets."

At the time of disbanding the army Congress was negligent in furnishing supplies or payment; the soldiers wished to make Washington the head of a monarchical government; he declined; then an appeal was secretly disseminated to officers to form a military despotism. Washington was informed of it. He called a meeting of the soldiers and his first words before unfolding the paper touched every heart. "You see, gentlemen," said he, as he placed his spectacles before his eyes, "that I have not only grown gray but blind in your service." It is needless to say that the mutiny was quelled. If the logic of war has not been sufficient to answer the old argument of State Rights, it would be well to re-read the history of those disjointed days and see if there were not previous to our Constitution sufficient need to "form a more perfect union." As we leave Newburgh Bay the broad rock close to the western shore is called "The Devils' Danskammer," or "The Devils' Dancing Chamber."

Directly opposite Newburgh are Matteawan and Fishkill. Hamburgh to the north is 69 miles from New York. The creek which here empties into the river is called Wappingers Creek. The residence of Governor George Clinton was one mile and a half from this place. The next place of importance is

POUGHKEEPSIE.

Queen City of the Hudson—the largest and most flourishing between New York and Albany. Standing midway between these cities, it presents many conveniences to the man of business, and its name—of Indian origin—(apokeepsing signifying safe harbor) is suggestive of pleasant homes and quiet retreats. The Hudson valley is rapidly becoming the "Central Park" of our country, and Poughkeepsie will always be one of its cool and shady spots. It is justly recognized as the finest residence city on the river, and the best writers in our country—gentlemen of extensive travel—give the name of "Sweet Home" to the Safe Harbor town! Safe Harbor, indeed, to the man weary with toil. *Safe Harbor* to the man of leisure and retirement; to the man who lives among his books and his friends; for in no place will we find a broader culture, more genial society, or warmer-hearted hospitality. And it is not only midway between the capital of our State and the metropolis of the continent, but it is also bounded by a historic and poetic horizon midway between the Highlands and the Catskills, commanding a view of the mountain portals on the south and the mountain overlook on the north—the Gibraltar of Revolutionary fame and the dream-land of Rip Van Winkle. The magnificent steamers which ply daily between New York and Albany, thirty trains on the best appointed railroad in the country, and fine steamers of home enterprise, make the traveling facilities complete. The city has a population of twenty-one thousand inhabitants, and every day advances with a steady growth. On our map of the Hudson we present two views—one taken from College Hill, a fine eminence about eight hundred feet above the river; the other from the opposite bank, with a view of the proposed Bridge—with a length of water span 2,420 feet, land approaches 1,080 feet, and height above water line 180 feet. We also present on our map a fine view of the Eastman Terrace. Mr. H. G. Eastman has been a live man in Poughkeepsie, and his grounds, always open to the public, are considered by citizens and visitors one of its chief attractions. This Terrace Block, just completed, fronts this magnificent park, and presents the finest terrace of suburban residences in the country. The Rev. Dr. Burchard, of New York, in his late article on the Hudson, says: "Their internal arrangements, from cellar to roof, are perfect. Their architectural facade and finish are beautiful. Their lawns and graveled walks and playing fountains are fascinating as the visions of a fairy land. Their occupants will overlook the finest scenery on earth. The far-off mountain, the nearer river in its extended flow and banks of unparalleled beauty; the queenly city, rising jeweled and crowned from her couch of emerald; and last, though not least, the classic grounds of the Professor, inclosed in walls of marble, undulating and adorned with park and fountain, and fowl of every feather, and orchards of luscious fruit, and vineyards of rarest vintage. Here is our ideal of a rural home. And what is most attractive, it can be obtained in fee simple for what the rent of an ordinary house in the city of New York would cost for only three or four years."

Any one who contemplates purchasing a pleasant home would do well to give a day's visit to the Homes and Drives of Poughkeepsie.

(RESIDENCE OF THE HON. H. G. EASTMAN.)

These Grounds are appropriately styled the "Central Park" of Poughkeepsie.

The drive to Hyde Park, to Vassar, along the south road, and the shady avenues, are among the finest.

Poughkeepsie has also every reason to feel proud of her institutions of learning. The Rev. D. G. Wright's Female Academy, pleasantly located in the central part of the city, is a school long distinguished for its excellent discipline. For thoroughness of instruction and carefulness of supervision, the academy is second to none in the "City of Schools." The buildings are ample and commodious, lighted throughout (except sleeping apartments) with gas, and warmed by hot air by furnaces in the basement. The rooms are large, well ventilated, and furnished with regard to taste, convenience, and comfort. The water, hot and cold, is conveyed to the second story, where there is a bathroom. The laboratory is furnished with an extensive philosophical, chemical, and astronomical apparatus. For literary and refined society, Poughkeepsie is unsurpassed, and this advantage has made it, as it were, the nucleus of schools in the Hudson River Valley. We present a cut of the Academy on the opposite page. For many years it has ranked among the first in our State in educational spirit and progress, and there is no place where young ladies can acquire a more healthy moral education, or a more finished and perfect symmetry in the development of mind and heart.

Just before the river boats land at Poughkeepsie we see upon our right, as we come up the river, a large structure, the "Riverview Military Academy." It crowns a fine eminence looking off toward the Highlands on the south, and the Catskills to the north and west. It is most thoroughly ventilated and heated by steam throughout. Water is accessible on every floor, and the room of each pupil is pleasant and commodious. The views are delightful in every direction, as will be seen from the cut here given. Mr. Bisbee has met with the most marked success in training boys for business, college, for West Point, and other military and naval institutions. In fact, he believes in an education which results in *force* of character—the true aim of all education.

Near the river we also see the extensive manufactory of Adriance, Platt & Co. In 1857 and 1858 this firm commenced the manufacture

POUGHKEEPSIE FEMALE ACADEMY.

and sale of the Buckeye Mower at Poughkeepsie, with sales-room in New York. The business has increased and enlarged in their hands materially, and they have attained such excellence in the manufacture of their machines that their reputation is world-wide. Twelve years have sufficed to extend the sale of the Buckeye from 25 machines to 30,000 in a single season. Surely the old chariots of war have become

RIVERVIEW MILITARY ACADEMY

A wide-awake thorough-going School for Boys wishing to be trained for Business, for College, or for West Point or the Naval Academy.

OTIS BISBEE, A. M., PRINCIPAL AND PROPRIETOR.

chariots of peace! Five miles north of Poughkeepsie is Hyde Park. The next place is Rhinecliff, where the Hudson River cars and boats land passengers for Rhinebeck, Rondout, and Kingston. Persons at Rondout take railroad to West Hurley, where stages connect with Overlook Mountain House, the description and cut of which is given in following pages.

VIEW ON THE HUDSON.

"Where every breeze breathes health and every sound is but the echo of tranquility."

THE NEW SUMMER RESORT.

OVERLOOK MOUNTAIN HOUSE.

VIA KINGSTON, ULSTER COUNTY, NEW YORK.

Ninety miles from New York, Sixty miles from Albany.

Take the Rondout and Oswego Railroad, from Rondout to West Hurley, (nine miles,) where the elegant carriages of Mr. Lasher, drawn by four horses, will be in readiness to convey you safely the remaining seven miles through a country romantic and beautiful. The "Overlook," a fine cut of which we present on the opposite page, is certainly "something new under the sun," and in fact a good deal *nearer* the sun than any Hotel along our River, being the highest peak of the Catskills and 3,800 feet above tide water. Every room in the Hotel presents a magnificent view, and from the public parlor, which is in the south end of the structure, one looking to the west and south sees mountain rising above mountain, while to the east the valley reaches away with its towns and villages to the blue hills of Connecticut and Massachusetts. And through this beautiful valley view of more than a hundred miles, the winding Hudson, fed by countless streams which make the meadows green, is reduced to a mere "Ribbon of Light."

Mountains without number rise on every hand—the named and the nameless,—from High Point in the south-west to Mount Holyoke in the east. The Hotel is 200 feet long by 36 feet wide, three stories high, French roof and basement, with a wing 54 feet long by 20 wide, and will easily accommodate 300 guests. A verandah 160 feet in length and 12 feet in width runs along the front of the Hotel. The grounds are tasty in arrangement, and the Hotel complete in all its appointments, including cold and hot water and gas throughout the house, daily mails and telegraph facilities.

NEW SUMMER RESORT.

OVERLOOK MOUNTAIN HOUSE.

Via Rondout and Kingston, Ulster County, N. Y.

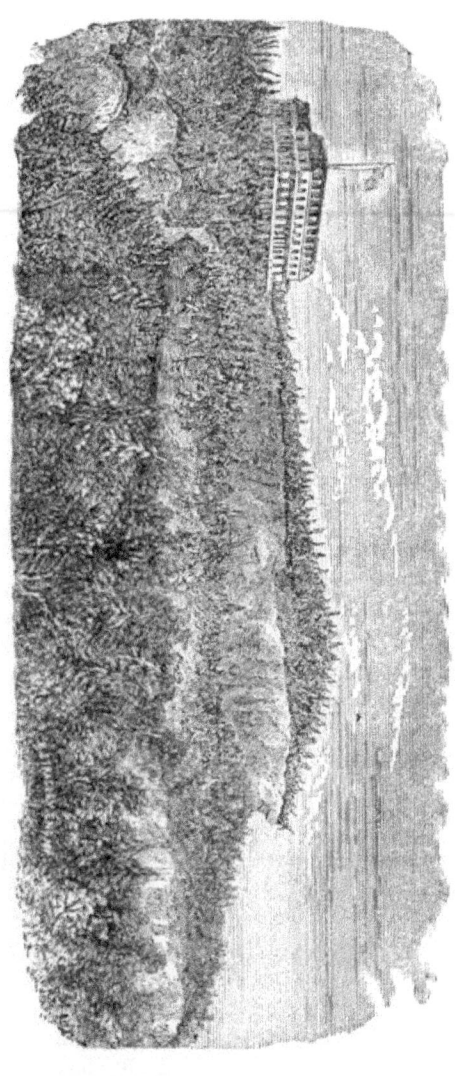

J. E. LASHER,

OVERLOOK MOUNTAIN HOUSE

WOODSTOCK P. O. N. Y.

CATSKILL.

The first that attracts our attention is the new hotel, "The Prospect Park Hotel," Breasted and Beach, proprietors. It was first opened to the public last season. They have been compelled to enlarge it to almost double its former capacity as completed last year. So that now the main building is two hundred and fifty feet front, with wing ninety feet by forty. There are three hundred and seventy feet of two-storied piazza, sixteen feet wide, supported by Corinthian pillars twenty-five feet high. From this piazza, whichever way you look, it seems as if the river lay at your feet. The plateau is two hundred and fifty feet above the river, and the grounds, seventeen acres in extent, are well adapted to the chief design. Guests can find either shade or sunshine, quiet or pleasure. To the north and northeast we see the Green Mountains of Vermont; to the South, the valley of the Hudson for thirty miles; the Man in the Mountain and the whole range of the Catskills. The fresh, bracing air from the mountain makes Catskill one of the pleasantest places to spend the heat of summer or the noontide of the year. And, indeed, a summer tour is not complete unless we pay the Catskill Mountains a visit. From the cliff in front of the "Mountain House," which looks out from the blue background of the mountains more than two thousand feet above the river, we get the finest panoramic view of the Hudson valley almost from the "wilderness to the sea." The Catskills are, moreover, the great *storehouse* of legends and traditions. They were called by the Indians the Onti-o-ra's, or Mountains of the Sky, as they sometimes seem like clouds along the horizon. This range of mountains was supposed by the Indians to have been originally a monster who devoured all the children of the Red Men, and that the Great Spirit touched him when he was going down to the salt lake to bathe, and here he remains. "Two little lakes upon the summit were regarded as the eyes of the monster, and these are open all the summer; but in the winter they are covered with a thick crust or heavy film; but whether sleeping or waking, tears always trickle down his cheeks. In these mountains, according to Indian belief, was kept the great treasury of storm and sunshine, presided over by an old squaw spirit who dwelt on the highest peak of the mountains. She kept day and night shut up in her wigwam, letting out only one at a time. She

PROSPECT PARK HOTEL,
CATSKILL, NEW YORK.

manufactured new moons every month, cutting up the old ones into stars, and, like the old Æolus of mythology, shut the winds up in the caverns of the hills." A morning view from this cliff will be remembered a lifetime; at least we remember, as if it were yesterday, a July morning three years ago. We rose at 3.30, at least an hour before

"Night murmured to the morning,—
Lie still, oh! love, lie still."

Patiently we waited the sun's advent, and as the rosy dawn announced the morning coming with "looks all vernal and with cheeks all bloom," the *windows* of the Mountain House, one after another, began to reveal undreamed visions of loveliness, and it were really difficult to tell which had the deeper interest, the sun's rising in the east, or the daughters in the west. The rosy clouds of the one, the tender blushes of the other; the opening eyelids of the morning, or the opening eyelids of innocence; the bright ambrosial locks hanging far and wide along the deep blue chiseled mountain side, or the *uncombed* ripples which, like mountain streams receiving additions from other sources, would probably become beautiful waterfalls. In four minutes more by solar time, and the sun would sprinkle the golden dust of light over the valley of the Hudson. The East was all aglow, and, *as we stood musing the fire burned*, yes, brighter and brighter, as if the distant hills were an altar, and a sacrifice was being offered up to the God of Day. It truly reminded one of an Oriental dry-goods store, with costly goods in the show-windows running opposition to the muslin and dimity-filled window-cases in the west.

Cities and villages below us sprang into being, and misty shapes rose from the valley, as if Day had rolled back the stone from the Sepulcher of Night, and it was rising transfigured to Heaven. Adown and up the river for the distance of sixty miles, sloops and schooners drifted lazily along, while below us the little

"ferry-boats plied
Like slow shuttles through the sunny warp
Of threaded silver from a thousand brooks."

Truly the Catskills were a fitting place for the artist Cole to gather inspiration to complete that beautiful series of paintings, "The Voyage

CATSKILL MOUNTAIN HOUSE.

of Life," for no finer mountains in all the world overlook a finer river. Irving, in writing of his first voyage up the Hudson, "in the good old times before steamboats and railroads had annihilated time and space, and driven all poetry and romance out of travel," says: "But of all the scenery of the Hudson the Kaatskill Mountains had the most witching effect on my boyish imagination. Never shall I forget the effect upon me of the first view of them, predominating over a wide extent of country,—part wild, woody, and rugged, part softened away into all the graces of cultivation. As we slowly floated along I lay on the deck and watched them through a long summer's day; undergoing a thousand mutations under the magical effects of atmosphere; sometimes seeming to approach; at other times to recede; now almost melting into hazy distance, now burnished by the setting sun, until in the evening they printed themselves against the glowing sky in the deep purple of an Italian landscape." On preceeding page we presented a cut of the Mountain House, furnished by Mr. C. L. Beach, proprietor. This favorite summer resort, so justly celebrated for its grand scenery and healthful atmosphere, will be open from June 1st to October 1st. Ready access may be had at all times by Mr. Beach's stages connecting at the village of Catskill with the Hudson River steamboats and the trains on the Hudson River Railroad. Two miles from the hotel are the Kaaterskill Falls. The waters fall perpendicularly 175 feet, and afterward 85 feet more. A sort of amphitheater behind the cascade is the scene of one of Bryant's finest poems:—

"From greens and shades where the Catterskill leaps
From cliffs where the wood flowers cling;"

and we recall the lines which express so beautifully the well-nigh fatal dream:—

"Of that dreaming one
By the base of that icy steep
When over his stiffening limbs begun
The deadly slumbers of frost to creep.
* * *
There pass the chasers of seal and whale,
With their weapons quaint and grim,
And bands of warriors in glittering mail,
And herdsmen and hunters huge of limb,
There are naked arms with bow and spear
And furry gauntlets the carbine rear.

About half-way up the mountain is the place said to be the dream-land of Rip Van Winkle—the greatest character of American Mythology, more real than the heroes of Homer or the massive gods of Olympus. And our age has reason to congratulate itself on the *possession* of Joseph Jefferson and John Rogers, who on the stage and in the studio have illustrated to the life this master-piece of Irving.

The cut here given repesents Rip Van Winkle at home, the favorite

of the village children. You will remember Irving says, "the children of the village would shout with joy whenever he approached, he assisted at their sports, made them playthings, taught them to fly kites and shoot marbles, and told them long stories of ghosts, witches and Indians. Whenever he went dodging about the village he was surrounded by a troop of them hanging on his skirts, clambering on his back and playing a thousand tricks on him with impunity." Two others complete the group, Rip Van Winkle on the mountains, and Rip Van Winkle returned. As will be seen above, the figure of Rip was modelled from Mr. Jefferson, who sat for his likeness. And as we turn away from the Catskills with their visions of beauty, and reality of fiction, we can only say, don't fail to hear the great actor when opportunity occurs, don't fail to read again the story of Irving, and don't fail to have the finest group of statuary in the world, price twelve dollars each. A stamp enclosed to John Rogers, 212 Fifth Avenue, will procure a fine illustrated catalogue and price list.

Six miles north of Catskill is Hudson, founded in the year 1784, by thirty persons from Providence, R. I. This is supposed to be the point where Hendrick Hudson anchored the 16th of September, 1609, and sent little boats up the river. The city has long enjoyed the reputation of hospitality, and strangers always receive a kindly welcome. Persons *en route* for Lebanon Springs take the Hudson and Boston Railroad to Chatham Village, and then the Harlem Extension up the beautiful Vale of Lebanon. Columbia Hall looks down from its hillside upon that beautiful valley which reminded Henry Vincent of the scenery of Llangollen in Wales. Persons *en route* for Pittsfield, at Chatham take the Boston and Albany, or drive from Lebanon Springs, a distance of seven miles. Pittsfield is a pleasant place, and the Grounds of the Maplewood Institute are very attractive, views of which are given on following pages.

Captain Powers line of steamers run daily from Hudson to New York. Athens is directly opposite, connected by ferry.

After leaving Hudson we pass Coxsackie on the left, a name of Indian origin; Stuyvesant on the right, named after Peter Stuyvesant; Kinderhook, five miles from the river, the home of Martin Van Buren; New Baltimore on the left; and two miles to the north Coeymans—named after one of the early inhabitants. The creek and neighborhood were originally called Hockatock. Directly opposite Coeymans is Schodack Landing, and four miles to the north, Castleton, with its pleasant church overlooking the river; and soon we see on our left the capital of New York. The buildings which at once attract our attention are the Cathedral, St. Joseph's Church, the domes of the State House and the City

Hall, and the statue of justice crowning the capitol. The new building is gradually progressing. It is to be hoped that they will preserve unharmed the statue of Justice which has so long been left out *in the cold*, and place it more in sight of the Legislature, in this way copying the worthy example of Charles the Fifth, or Frederick, who had such a statue in the window that he might always have Justice in view. Albany was once called Bever-wyck, and Wiliamstadt. The Dutch first established a trading post on Castle Island immediately below the present site of

DELAVAN HOUSE.

Albany, 1614. Fort Aurania was erected where the city now stands, 1623. Its present name was given in honor of the Duke of Albany, in 1664, on the surrender of the fort to the English. The Indians called it Shaunaugh-ta-da, or "once the pine plains." The State Library, the Geological Rooms, and Medical School will repay a visit. The finest hotel by far, is the "Delavan," by Charles E. Leland, also proprietor of the "Clarendon Hotel" in Saratoga. Folsom's Business College located here, is one of the most thorough in the country. The "People's Line," and also the magnificent day boats—the *Vibbard* and the *Drew*—

MAPLEWOOD INSTITUTE FOR YOUNG LADIES, PITTSFIELD, MASS.,

Has beautiful and spacious grounds; the largest, finest, and oldest School Gymnasium in the United States; unsurpassed Literary and Artistic advantages; and a high and well-established reputation, which has long attracted patrons and pupils from all parts of the Country.

Rev. C. V. SPEAR, Principal.

ply between New York and Albany. The principal streets are North and South Broadway, State street, North and South Pearl, and Washington avenue. The principal buildings are the State Geological and Agricultural Hall, the Capitol buildings, New York State Library, and Dudley Observatory. It might also be well to notice that this was one of the towns honored by the "Cardiff Giant." He laid in state for a number of days at the Geological Rooms, a remarkable specimen of the *naked* truth in a good state of preservation :

"Weep for Adonais! He is dead."

The Albany Cathedral is a fine structure. The iron fence about it, made at the "Albany Iron and Machine Works," is probably the finest work of its kind in the United States. The railing also on the new Bridge across the Hudson at Albany is of their manufacture, to which we call the respectful attention of all who have a taste for art and beauty in this "age of iron." These works, known all over the country, were established in 1847 by Stark & Pruyn. They were succeeded by the well-known firm of Pruyn & Lansing, in whose hands they remained until 1867, when the present energetic proprietor, Henry C. Haskell, came into possession. He has recently erected a new building, near the Steamboat Landing, and the Depot of the Albany and Susquehanna Railroad, four stories high, fifty feet by sixty, which increases his facilities of doing with promptness and dispatch his continually increasing business.

TROY.

Going north from Albany, we come to Troy, at the head of tide water, the enterprising city of the Hudson. In fact, it might be considered the *live* town of the river. In the year 1786 it was called Ferryhook. In 1787 Rensselaerwyck. In the fall of 1787 the settlers began to use the name of Vanderheyden, named after the family who owned a great part of the ground where the city now stands. January 9, 1789, the freeholders of the town met and gave it the name of Troy. As a natural sequence the adjoining hills took the classical names of Ida and Olympus.

The large Iron and Steel Rail Works are in the southern part of the city. The manufactory of Waters's Patent Paper Boats is about a mile and a half from their office, River street. These boats are acquiring a world-wide reputation, and certainly need no better recommendation than the fact that they are used by Brown, Coulter, and Hamill. During the last four seasons these boats have been rowed by the winners of more than a hundred matched races.

Stearns' "Mansion House" is a large, pleasant, and convenient hotel, located in the central and business part of the town, opposite the steamboat landing, and only two or three minutes' walk from the depot.

During the last two or three years many fine, substantial blocks have been built, showing at once public spirit and private enterprise.

MAPLE AVENUE.
Grounds of Maplewood Institute, Pittsfield, Mass.

NIAGARA FALLS, ST. LAWRENCE, AND MONTREAL.

AT the unveiling of Shakespeare's monument in Central Park William Cullen Bryant said, what Niagara is to other waterfalls, Shakespeare is to other poets. As this embraces in one sentence its greatness and grandeur, we will proceed forthwith in our route from Albany to that ever-veiled crowning glory of our continent. From New York there are three pleasant routes to Albany. The magnificent Day Line of steamers, the C. Vibbard and the Daniel Drew; the Albany and Troy Night Line of steamers; and the Hudson River Railroad. This Railroad route, without change to Niagara, furnished with drawing-room cars and Pullman coaches, combines speed with the greatest comfort. In fact, our times have outgrown the inconveniences of travel. The dream of Arabian fancy is realized. These sumptuous saloons remind one of the "enchanted carpet" which wafted the traveler from place to place. Starting, then, from Albany, which we presume is already reached by one of these three routes, we take the *New York Central Railroad*, pass Dudley Observatory on the left, and soon leave the domes of the river-crowned Capitol behind us. Passing through Schenectady, Fonda, Palatine Bridge, Fort Plain, and places of minor interest, we come to Little Falls—the head-centre of Herkimer cheese. Here the *gentle* Mohawk of the poet rushes through a rock channel of remarkable formation, and we come to the conclusion that the writer of "How sweet is the vale where the Mohawk gently glides," was not a native of Herkimer. We get a good view of river and rocks from the car windows. A few miles further bring us to Utica, the first express station from Albany, and one of the most flourishing cities in central New York, built on rising ground. This was the site of old Fort Schuyler. Passengers for Trenton Falls and Richfield Springs here change cars; for the Falls, take the Utica and Black River Railroad to South Trenton—whole distance from Albany, 105 miles. These falls are six in number, viz: Sherman's Fall, with a descent of thirty-five feet; Conrad's Fall, twenty-one feet; High Falls, one hundred and nine feet; Mill Dam and Upper Falls, respectively, seventeen and twenty-one feet; and the Cascades, about eighteen feet. These Falls are well worthy a visit, for, besides their own intrinsic beauty, the scenery on the banks and cliffs is wild and romantic, and materially enhances their grandeur. The attractions in and about Utica will well repay a few days' visit. Probably there is no city which even the passing stranger holds in better remembrance, as this furnishes

THE BUTTERFIELD HOUSE, UTICA, N. Y.

the best Restaurant on the line of the Central Railroad. All trains stop ten minutes, and many pass by the eating-house at Albany to save an appetite for "ten minutes at Utica." Mr. D. M. Johnson, the proprietor, is also proprietor of the finest Hotel in the city—the "Butterfield House"—a few blocks removed from the noise and turmoil of the Depot. A cut of the Hotel is here given. It is complete in every particular, and is situated in the central and business part of the city. Free omnibuses to and from the cars. The next place of importance is

Rome, where the Central connects with the Rome, Watertown and Ogdensburgh line. This makes a pleasant trip to Montreal down the St. Lawrence; and also there is a line (the Vermont Central) direct from Ogdensburgh to St. Albans, the White and Green Mountains. Syracuse is the next city of importance on the New York Central. This is a fine city, enterprising and flourishing, and almost as well salted as old Sodom and Gomorrah, the cities of the plain. Here are railroad connections with Binghamton and Oswego, and here also the old and new Central diverges, meeting again at Rochester. The New road, over which the through trains pass, takes in Clyde, Lyons, and Palmyra; the Old road, Auburn, Seneca Falls, Geneva, Clifton Springs, and Canandaigua. (Persons *en route* for Watkins Glen can change cars at Geneva, and take the steamboat on Seneca Lake, or take cars at Canandaigua.) These two lines come together at Rochester, the finest city of Western New York, if not the finest in the State. It is situated on the Genesee River, which we cross as we come into the city, and get a view on our right of the falls where Sam Patch made his last leap. The best hotel is the Osborn House, centrally located. Passing through Brockport, Albion, Medina, and Lockport, we come to Niagara, and making our way through throngs of porters and carriages, whose clamor drowns even the roar of waters, we find ourselves safely and quietly located in the pleasant rooms of the International—appropriately named, for scenery like Niagara, even if Canada were a part of our country, could never belong to one nation or people. It is *International*. It belongs to the world. This hotel, under the supervision of Mr. James T. Fulton, owner and proprietor, has won a wide reputation for its civility and attention to guests. And now being comfortably located, we will proceed to take a look at the "scenery." A few steps bring us to the American Falls (900 feet across, and 164 feet high). We have all seen pictures of these falls, from Church's masterpiece to the hastily engraved cut of a Guide Book. In short, we all have an idea how the falls *look;* but they never *speak* to us until we have looked over that deep abyss, and up the stream which ever rushes on like a great army to battle, and miles down the crowded channel where the black waters have worn their passage, through the silent, unknown centuries. Remember what they say to you, oh, hearer! and as you look upon them the first time uncover your head a single moment. The *language* is addressed to your soul. One-eighth of a mile below these falls is the new Suspension Bridge, the longest in the world—1300 feet in length, the towers 100 feet high, and cables 1800 feet long. This carriage and foot-way was long needed, and now not only presents a fine view of the Falls from every stand-point, but affords the most convenient route to the views on the Canada side. It was opened to the public January 4th, 1869. Goat Island, the natural Central Park of the Falls, is connected with the American side by a bridge. The area of the island is about sixty acres. In our hasty sketch we will, however, only name the places to be visited, leaving the description to the local guide books. The Cave of the Winds, with its magnificent curtain of changing beauty, the Rainbow, the Whirlpool Rapids, reached by the Double Elevator. Terrapin Bridge and Prospect Tower, overlooking Horse Shoe Falls (about 1900 feet wide and 158 feet high). On the Canada side the principal points of interest are Table Rock and the broad Causeway, where one can feel all the glory of Niagara, and where Mrs. Sigourney wrote those expressive lines—

> "God has set
> His rainbow on thy forehead, and the clouds
> Mantled around thy feet."

Burning Spring is about a mile above Table Rock, near the river edge. Not far from this the battle of Chippewa was fought, July 5, 1814. And also, a mile and a half from the falls, is the battle ground of Lundy's Lane. The Suspension Bridge, two miles below, is a triumph in art; the Whirlpool is about a mile below this bridge. Many writers have attempted to describe Niagara, but in every description there is something lacking. We can give its dimensions, its height and breadth, and point out the places to be seen; but there is a *Unity* about Niagara which can only be felt. It makes one wish that David could have seen it, and added a new chapter to the Psalms. It surely would not have been out of place in the chapter following "The heavens declare the glory of God, the firmament showeth His handiwork." In happy reminiscence the great English novelist has perhaps written its best description: "I think in every quiet season, now, still do these waters roll, and leap, and roar, and tumble, all day long. Still are the rainbows spanning them, a hundred feet below. Still, when the sun is on them, do they shine and glow like molten gold. Still, when the day is gloomy, do they fall like snow, or seem to crumble away like the front of a great chalk cliff, or roll down the rock like dense white smoke. But always does the mighty stream appear to die as it comes down, and always from the unfathomable grave arises that tremendous ghost of spray and mist which is never laid, which has haunted the place with the same dread solemnity since darkness brooded on the deep, and that first flood before the deluge—Light—came rushing on Creation at the word of God."

Tourists making the round trip to Montreal, Lake Champlain, Lake George, Saratoga, and New York, or the still longer round trip to Montreal, the Green and White Mountains *ria* Boston or Portland to New York, have *two routes* to Montreal—one *ria* the Grand Trunk Railroad, the other *ria* boat down the Lake and the St. Lawrence. If you go *ria* boat, take cars to Lewiston, a town on the American side, about opposite Queenston, and a few miles brings us to the Lake. Taking a good night's rest on the Lake, we arrive at Kingston in the morning, and six miles below Kingston we are among the "Thousand Islands" of the St. Lawrence. These islands, in reality about 1800, extend forty miles. The largest is Grande, or Wolf Island.

At Ogdensburgh persons may take the Vermont Central Railroad, 118 miles to St. Albans, and go to Montreal, Boston, and south or east, or continue the route by the Rapids to Montreal. About five miles below Ogdensburgh we have the first rapid around an islet called Chimney Island; next, the rapids of the Long Sault, nine miles in length. Here the river runs twenty miles an hour; then the Coteau Rapids, below Grand Island; then the Lachine Rapids, below the town of La Chine; and nine miles bring us to Montreal. Montreal is 540 miles from the

Gulf of St. Lawrence, 186 miles south-west from Quebec, and 420 miles from New York. It is situated on the south side of an island thirty miles in length, and ten miles in greatest breadth. Mount Royal, from which it took its name, is 1000 feet in height. The Victoria Bridge, often called the eighth wonder of the world, is an iron tube two miles in length, resting on 24 piers. Montreal is well called the City of Churches. The Cathedral of No re Dame, capable of seating from 10,000 to 12,000 people, with its twin towers and Gothic architecture, somewhat resembles "our Mother Church," on the banks of the Seine. In one of these towers is a chime of bells; in the other, the largest bell in the Western Continent, weighing fourteen tons. The paintings in the Church of the Jesuits are magnificent. St. Patrick's and many others will repay a visit. The quays of the city are the finest on the continent. The Ottawa is in reality the pleasantest Hotel of Montreal. It is more thoroughly "United States" in its character—a sufficient recommendation to foreigners or Americans. It has been thoroughly refitted and refurnished; the tables are covered with the best plate and silver ware; and, what is still better, the substantials and luxuries of the season. Among the different mercantile establishments we would mention Savage, Lyman & Co., Jewelers, house established in 1818; and the famous Recollet House, Brown & Claggett proprietors. There is a marked civility of Montreal citizens toward strangers, and every one carries from the island city the pleasantest of recollections.

From Montreal persons go *via* Vermont Central to St. Albans, Mount Mansfield, and the White Mountains, connecting with the Passumpsic Railroad at White River Junction. Persons *en route* for New York take the cars at Montreal *via* St. Albans and Rutland, or *via* Rouse's Point, Plattsburgh, and Lake Champlain. Persons would be well repaid to stop over a day at St. Albans—a town of about 5,000 inhabitants, made famous during the Rebellion by a Canadian raid. The village is situated about two miles from, and overlooks Lake Champlain; the view from the hill to the east is hardly equaled in New England. The Lake with its islands, the broad valleys, and far away the peaks of the Adirondacks. Here is the large and magificent hotel, the "Welden House."

Its reputation as a pleasant and attractive place of summer resort, as well as an agreeable and comfortable house at all times for travelers, is not surpassed in New England. It contains over two hundred rooms, and is admirably arranged for private families.

"The panoramic views from St. Albans are among the finest in th world. Aldis Hill, spoken of in 'Norwood,' is within one-half mile of

THOMAS LAVENDER, PROPRIETOR.

the Welden House, and the summit of Bellevue, accessible by an easy carriage road, is within two miles, commanding on the east a view of Mansfield and Jay, besides a wide reach of mountain, valley, hill, and plain, adorned with lovely farms and villages; on the west a magnificent view of the Adirondacks, besides a hundred miles of Lake Champlain, dotted with sails, broken with islands, and bounded by a wide stretch of as lovely a country as the eye ever beheld; while on the north the vision rests on Canada, the Richelieu and St. Lawrence Rivers.

International Hotel,

AMERICAN SIDE,

J. T. FULTON, Proprietor,

NIAGARA FALLS.

THE

Largest and Most Pleasantly Situated Hotel at Niagara,

AND NEARER TO THE FALLS THAN ANY OTHER HOUSE.

ROOMS LARGE AND WELL VENTILATED.

Spacious Piazzas and Magnificent Lawn and Croquet Ground attached.

ACCOMMODATIONS FOR 600 GUESTS.

Parties can be furnished at all times with Rooms low down, single or in suits as may be desired.

All the Modern Improvements in the Building.

Everything strictly first-class, and terms reasonable. Every attention guaranteed.

OMNIBUSSES AND PORTERS AT ALL TRAINS.

RAIL ROAD, STEAMBOAT AND TELEGRAPH OFFICES IN THE HOTEL.

OTTAWA HOTEL.

C. S. BROWNE, Manager.

This Popular First-Class Hotel accommodates 400 Guests.

The OTTAWA HOTEL covers the entire space of ground running between St. James and Notre Dame Streets, and has two beautiful fronts: the one on the right, in the above cut, represents the front on Notre Dame Street—the other on the left, the St. James Street front. The house has been thoroughly **Refitted** and **Furnished**, with every regard to comfort and luxury—has Hot and Cold Water, with Baths and Closets on each floor. The aim has been to make this the most UNEXCEPTIONABLE FIRST-CLASS HOTEL IN MONTREAL.

The Manager respectfully informs the travelling public, that he intends by constant attention to the wants of his patrons, to make this hotel a comfortable home for travellers.

THE OTTAWA HOTEL is the only First-class Hotel in the City kept on the American plan. ☞ Carriages, with attentive drivers, may be had at all times by application at the Office.

Coaches will also be found at the Railway Depot, and Steamboat Landings, on the arrival of the several Trains and Steamers.

The Montreal Telegraph Company have an Office in the Hotel.

Persons *en route* for Quebec take either the Grand Trunk Railway, or by steamer down the St. Lawrence. This city goes by the name of the "Ancient Capitol"—triangular in form, and divided into the Upper and Lower Town. It is the best specimen of an ancient town on the continent, and one of the finest "walled cities" in the world. It is also interesting as a historic point. It was taken by the British and Colonial forces in 1720, restored to France in 1732, finally captured by Wolfe in 1759, and together with all the French possessions in North America added to Great Britain at the peace of 1763. Quebec is 400 miles from the sea, and the tide rises and falls 20 feet. Down the river from Quebec are the beautiful falls of Montmorenci, 250 feet high, and 50 wide. Excursions are also made to the Saguenay River. From Quebec the southern route takes us *via* Lake Memphremagog and Wells River to the White Mountains, the Crawford House, the Twin Mountain, the Profile, and the ascent of Mount Washington by the Elevated Railway, and so to Lake Winnepiseogee, to Conway and Boston, or *via* the Connecticut Valley to New York.

TOURISTS WILL FIND

The best Summer and Winter Stereoscopic views of

NIAGARA FALLS,

AT

Mr. GEORGE BARKERS,

Opposite the Cataract House.

1500 DISTINCT VIEWS.

ALSO, INDIAN WORK AND CURIOSITIES.

SARATOGA SPRINGS.

This great watering place of the *continent* is reached from New York *via* the Hudson River boats to Albany or Troy, and thence by Rensselaer and Saratoga Railroad, or *via* Hudson River cars without change in less than six hours. From Niagara *via* Central Railroad to Schenectady, and thence *via* Rensselaer and Saratoga Railroad. From Montreal *via* Plattsburgh and Lake Champlain, or through St. Albans direct by cars over the Vermont Central and Rensselaer and Saratoga from Rutland. From White Mountains, either by way of Burlington or Bellows Falls

PARK OF THE GRAND UNION HOTEL.

and Rutland. From Boston *via* Cheshire, or Boston and Albany Railroads. From Manchester, Vt., and the Green Mountains, *via* Rutland, or *via* Bennington and Troy. Saratoga is a city of hotels. Probably no town or city in the world has three so large and so near together; the Grand Union, the Congress, and the Grand Central. The Grand Union capable of accommodating about eighteen hundred guests, is

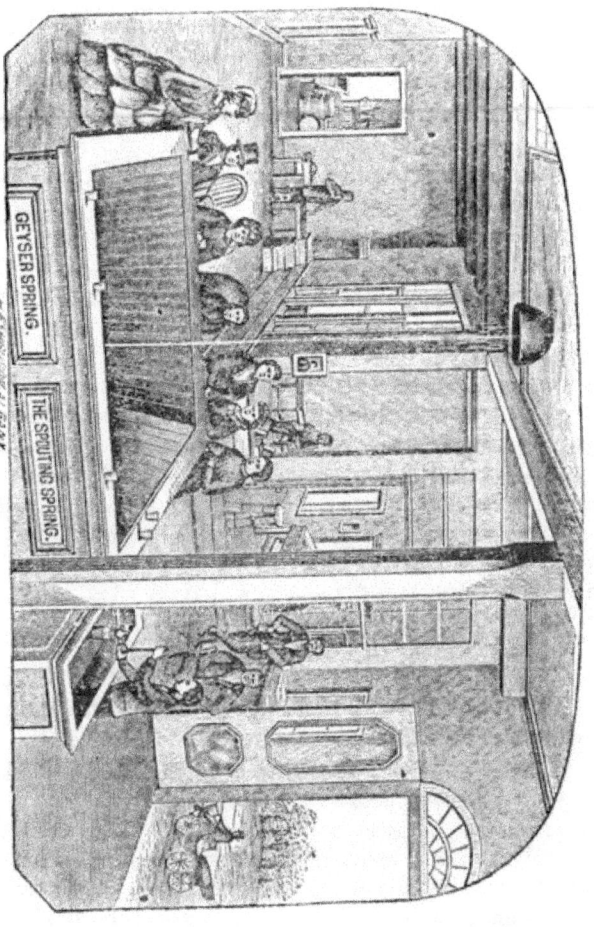

GEYSER SPRING, SARATOGA.

conducted by Breslin, Gardner & Co., the enterprising proprietors of the Gilsie House, New York. The buildings are arranged in the form of a quadrangle, enclosing a beautiful park, a view of which is here given. The Congress is almost opposite. The Grand Central, separated by a street on the right. The Clarendon enjoys the advantage of a fine location, overlooking the park and its proprietor, Charles E. Leland, of the Delavan House, Albany, has a host of warm and genuine friends. The springs resemble the hotels in at least one particular. They are almost innumerable, and most of them a success. The Congress, the Star, the Hathorn, the Geyser, the High Rock, the Seltzer, &c., are all widely known. The Star forwards in barrels water to all parts of the country, and retains all its properties equal to any water that is bottled. The great "curiosity" of Saratoga is the Geyser or Spouting Spring. It is situated about one mile and a half southwest of Saratoga Springs, in the "Cocesa Valley," near the railroad and carriage road to Ballston Spa. Appearances of mineral waters had been observed here for some years, and at last Messrs. Vail & Seavey, the proprietors of a factory located at that point, determined to sink a shaft in search of a spring. After boring 140 feet, the shaft penetrated the cavern that concealed the hidden treasure, and from its contracted prison-house the water spouted forth several feet from the top of the shaft. The well was then tubed, and from this spring a continual stream of mineral water issues, and rises some 20 or 25 feet in the air. It is well worth visiting, this being the only spring in Saratoga which has presented this phenomenon.

The fact that the spring is located beneath a solid rock of 140 feet in thickness, renders it free from all impurities of surface waters, which accounts for its uniform taste and clearness.

Lines of stages run every two hours between the principal hotels and the spring for the accommodation of visitors.

Seven miles south of Saratoga is the pleasant village of Ballston Spa, and the well-known Sans Souci Hotel. Here also are the Ballston Artesian Lithia Spring, the Franklin, and the new Sans Souci in the hotel grounds. From Saratoga excursions are also made to the Lake and Luzerne, a pretty little village at the junction of the Sacandaga and the Hudson.

LAKE GEORGE.

From New York, via river boats or cars, to Albany or Troy; thence via Rensselaer and Saratoga Railroad to Glen's Falls. From which point stages run direct to the Fort William Henry Hotel, on the Lake. The Rensselaer and Saratoga Railroad, always awake to the comfort and wants of the people, built (1870) a branch from Fort Edward to

THE ROCKWELL HOUSE, GLEN'S FALLS.

Glen's Falls, making the route much pleasanter than formerly. The town of Glen's Falls is the most flourishing and enterprising in Northern New York. The streets are finely laid out and well shaded. The Soldiers' Monument and the new Music Hall testify to the taste, intelligence, and public spirit of the place.

The Rockwell House, just completed, a cut of which is here given, is quite as complete in all its appointments as any hotel in the State. The rooms are all spacious and airy, and an atmosphere of home and comfort pervades the entire establishment. The gentlemanly proprietors, the Rockwell Brothers, are well known among tourists and travelers. Educated in this "art of arts" by one who has made our own *Luzerne*, at the meeting of the Sacandaga and the Hudson, quite as well known and reverently regarded as the classic Luzerne of Switzerland. Conveyances can be had at all times to Lake George, and stages leave morning and evening. Persons arriving on the evening train thus have a good night's rest, and a pleasant morning ride to the Lake. Glen's Falls is surrounded by so much of historic interest and beautiful scenery that it demands even from the hurried traveler more than a passing glance. This is the central point, as it were, about which our great novelist grouped the scenes of "The Last of the Mohicans." A short distance from the village the Hudson River makes a descent of 72 feet in a succession of leaps over rugged rocks; and here is the famous cave so graphically described by Cooper. The width of the river at this point is about 900 feet.

A fine plank road connects Glen's Falls with the Lake, passing through a beautiful country. It is well built and always smooth, and seems like a highway to some city rather than an excursion route for summer travel. On the way we pass Bloody Pond, on the right, and a monument to Col. Williams, on the left. Lake George is a place where one goes with the idea of staying two or three days, and then— stays two or three weeks. The charming scenery and cheerful Hotel (the Fort William Henry) present perhaps the strongest combination to be found in our country of immediate beauty and comfort. Near the Hotel are the ruins of old Fort William Henry, telling a sad history of the past. About a mile to the south-east are the ruins of Fort George. It has been christened about as many times as the Hudson, and like the Hudson has retained its prosiest name. The Iroquois called it Audiata-rocte (the lake that shuts itself in); by other tribes Canidere-oit (the tail of the Lake, as a part of Lake Champlain). Father Jaques, traversing it in 1646, during the festival of Corpus

FORT WILLIAM HENRY HOTEL, LAKE GEORGE.

T. ROESELLE & SON, PROPRIETORS.

ALSO OF THE

Arlington House, Washington, D. C.

Christi, called it Lac Sacrament. Sir William Johnson, serving his king with greater zeal than his country, styled it Lake George. Its most poetical name was Horicon—of uncertain origin, said to signify silvery water. Lake George combines various attractions. It has something of interest for every one—the lover of history, of romance, of beauty, and lovers generally (as a friend remarks, not confined to inanimate objects). But we believe the greatest attraction is in the unwritten poetry which lives among these scattered islands. A graceful little steamboat makes a daily trip to and from Ticonderoga. The islands are said to be the same in number as the days of the year, and we think one might find a small rock extra for leap year.

PRINCIPAL ISLANDS.

Two miles down the Lake Tea Island, next Diamond; Long Island, 12 miles from Caldwell; Dome Island, Recluse Island. After Bolton Landing we come to "14-mile Island;" Shelving Rock on the east, and Tongue Mountain opposite. (These form the entrance to the Narrows.) This is the most picturesque portion of the Lake; it is at this place 400 feet deep. Sabbath Day Point, (where Gen. Abercrombie landed, on his way to attack the French one Sabbath morning), Bluff Point, Odell Island, Scotch Bonnet, Anthony's Nose, on the east; and Rogers' Slide on the west.

Saratoga Star Spring Co.

THE SARATOGA STAR SPRING CO. have demonstrated by actual use that the waters from their Spring will keep for Months in their bbls., which are lined with pure tin, and hold its properties as well as in bottles. They now have half bbls. (15 gallons,) being an equivalent of three cases water, which they will lend to customers free of charge, provided they are returned freight paid, and will sell the water at Four Dollars per half bbl. Being less than one-fifth the cost of the same amount of water in pt. bottles, and can be transported for about the price of one case.

Customers can avail themselves of this method of dispensing the water by applying to the Star Spring Co.

PRICE.

Water in half bbls. - - $4 for 16 gals.
Water in qt. bottles, 2 *dozen in Case*, $5 per Case.
Water in pt. " 4 " " $7 per Case.
Water in bbls. to dealers (*equivalent to six Cases*) $7.50.

Address

SARATOGA STAR SPRING CO.,
SARATOGA. NEW YORK

MELVIN WRIGHT, Supt. and Gen. Agt.

One of the interesting features of Albany is the celebrated Clothing House of Davis & Co. No one should leave the city without paying it

a visit. If tourists want anything in their line, they will be honorably dealt by. We can recommend the Establishment in every particular.

DELAWARE AND HUDSON CANAL COMPANY.

ALBANY AND SUSQUEHANNA RAILROAD DEPARTMENT.

There are few Railroads in our country that possess for so many miles such variety and interest as the Albany & Susquehanna. All the way from Albany to Binghamton the hills and valleys, the streams, rivulets, and rivers form a succession of beautiful landscapes framed in the moving panorama of a car window. The railroad follows the valleys of three streams—the Schoharie, the Cobleskill, and the Susquehanna. Leaving Albany we pass through the little villages and stations of Adamsville, Slingerlands, New Scotland, Guilderland, Knowersville, Duanesburgh, Quaker Street, and come to Esperance, thirty-one miles from Albany. The site of this village was bought by General William North in 1800, and named by him Esperance, a French word signifying Hope. Incorporated April 21, 1832. The next station, Central Bridge, thirty-six miles from Albany, is the Junction with the branch road for Schoharie Courthouse and Middleburgh. Schoharie village, the county seat, is situated on Schohaire Flats. First settlement was made in 1711. Population about fifteen hundred. The old stone church, erected in 1772, is now used as an arsenal. Three miles from Central Bridge, or thirty-nine miles from Albany, is the celebrated

HOWE'S CAVE.

This cave was discovered on the 22d May, 1842, by Lester Howe. From the kind of rock and various cavernous indications he imagined there was a large cave in the vicinity, and for more than a year searched diligently for an opening. His conjectures were certainly more than realized, for even in his wildest dreams he little thought that he should find a new world of beauty, with arches and walls reaching away for miles, of which, perhaps, the half is only discovered. When the entrance was discovered the passage-way was almost completely closed for almost a mile with gravel, clay, and rocks. By closing the side water-courses these obstructions were washed away, which otherwise it would have taken years to remove; even as Hercules *in one day* cleaned the celebrated Augean stables (where three thousand oxen had dined for thirty years), by leading through them the waters of the Alpheus and the Peneus. We occasionally, even in our practical days, see the disregarded classics taking common sense by the hand and extending her congratulations. Every one who goes once is so enthusiastic in praise of these hidden secrets as seen in the light of science and the *light of oil*, that every year the tide of travel increases for the "Cave."

The best time for a visit is said to be from June to October. Between these months persons may pass in three or four miles and return without being wet by a drop of water. According to the Description of the Cave, published some time ago, "the direction of the main cave varies from north to northwest, but the branches pass in all directions. The strata through which the cave passes dips slightly to the south. The water always flows toward the entrance of the main cave, but the whole of it is discharged by the side passages, except during the high water of spring. The temperature of the air is said to be uniformly at 48 Fh. at the distance of half a mile from the entrance at all times of the year."

Having put ourselves into proper apparel for the *voyage*, we pass down a flight of stairs bringing the explorer to the entrance, which is almost twelve feet in height, with an average width of seven or eight feet. This is the real starting-point, and the effect of each person with a gimbal lamp always right side up with care or carelessness, and the uncouth garments "clinging like cerements," are certainly ludicrous and grotesque. Miss Logan, Miss Dickinson, and Mrs. Stanton could wear pants here with propriety. Every one does. Custom and convenience alike require it. The first room is styled the Subterranean Lecture Room, six to ten feet in height and forty feet wide in widest place. The next room is Washington Hall—and here it is said that sometimes the mythical king of this subterranean world addresses visitors as follows. We can only take the matter as reported, prefacing it, however, with this idea, that either the Reporter is decidedly florid in his style, or else this subterranean king must have taken lessons in rhetoric at Harvard or Ann Arbor. For fuller report, see the "Description of Howe's Cave, with a popular treatise on the formation of Caves in Lime Rock, from the size of a quill to a mammoth."

YE ADDRESS OF YE SUBTERRANEAN.

"My alien friends, from all parts of the world above, I always welcome your visits through my dominions. My country, no less than yours, abounds in strange and wonderful things. Whether you look above or below, to the right or to the left, every scene is a page in the natural history of my empire; but whether you are to read a page or a volume is a problem to be solved only by your own close attention and study. . . . Open, then, your eyes, that you may see and understand, and thus obtain the trophies by which you will be surrounded in your journey through every part of my empire: take them to the land of your domicile, and there bear in mind that your torch will shine none the less bright from having lighted your neighbor's," and so on to the end of the chapter.

The next room is Washington Hall, from six to twenty-five feet high; next the Bridal Chamber (temperature 48 Fh.) where many have been nuptially tied, including the two daughters of the Discoverer. Next comes the Wine Room and the Chapel, some forty feet high; then Harlem Tunnel and Cataract Hall; then Pool of Siloam; the Indian Stone Ladder; Franklin Avenue; Flood Hall; Congress Hall; the Ghost Room and Haunted Castle; Music Hall and Stygian Lake, one fourth of a mile in length, where we embark for Plymouth Rock; passing through the Devil's Gangway we come to the Museum, the Geological Rooms, Uncle Tom's Cabin, the Giant's Study, his *Nursery* for Young Giants, the Pirate's Cave, the Rocky Mountains, the Valley of Jehosaphat, which takes one back 3,000 years to the building of the Temple; the Winding Way and the Rotunda, a high, round chamber whose height has never been measured. We are only able to mark out the route in this hasty manner. To speak of all the objects of interest would draw us aside from the purpose of a general guide. It is something to be seen and felt rather than described. The hand of nature has fashioned curiously these walls; stalactites and stalagmites of almost every form adorn many of the rooms. Here hangs a harp of exquisite finish; here are columns, arches, and niches, and statues, too, like Tennyson's Godiva, "clad in chastity." Every one should visit Howe's Cave and see these real Arabian Night beauties so near the capital of the Empire State. The next station is Cobleskill, forty-five miles from Albany and ten miles westerly from Schoharie Court House. This rich and fertile valley was called by the Indians Ots-ga-ra-ga. The village is one of the most thriving and flourishing on the route, and here is Smith's National Hotel, A. C. Smith, proprietor, one of the best on the line, and decidedly the best in the place. Here is the Junction of the Cherry Valley, Sharon, and Albany Railroad, which passes through Hyndsville and Seward to Sharon Springs, fourteen miles from Cobleskill and nine miles beyond Sharon to Cherry Valley, its terminus.

UNION HOTEL, SHARON SPRINGS,
ANDREAS WILLMAN, Proprietor.

SHARON SPRINGS,
"The Rose of Sharon and the Lily of the Valley" for 1871. Who?

One of the oldest and one of the most satisfactory summer resorts of our country. The village is splendidly located, as it has been said, *in a valley on a hill*. The streets are well shaded. There are nine large hotels, always full. One of the pleasantest of these in location and every point of comfort, is the "Union Hotel," a cut of which has been given. The cool and shaded verandas, the large and well-furnished rooms, and every luxury in its season, combine to make it the place to spend a summer season. The picturesque scenery of Sharon and environs, and the beautiful Park Promenades and Drives have made this Summer Resort one of the most frequented in the United States.

Since the completion of the Branch Railroad from Cobleskill, it is very easy of access, *via* the Hudson boats or Hudson River Railroad, only about two hours' from Albany, by the Albany and Susquehanna Railroad. The long stage road is now avoided. Sharon is widely celebrated for its Sulphur, Magnesia, and Chalybeate springs; and they have, and justly deserve, a high reputation for the cure of cutaneous diseases. There is also a new and commodious hotel situated on the Heights, one half mile from the waters, Fethers' Hotel, C. B. Fethers proprietor, where a person can get pure mountain air, large and handsomely furnished apartments, and excellent board at low rates. This hotel is kept open summer and winter, and is the nearest to the station. Carriages to and from the dépôt and springs free of charge. The next station on this branch road is Cherry Valley, where there is a pleasant summer resort, "The Park House." This town is in the northeast corner of Otsego county. Mount Independence southeast of the center, is a rocky eminence 1.000 feet above the valleys, and 2,000 feet above tide water. Tek-ah-ra-wa Falls are on a small creek in the north part of the town, about 160 feet in height. Returning now to Cobleskill, the next station west on the line of the Albany and Susquehanna is Richmondville, a village of about 500 inhabitants, lying below us on the left of the road. Passing through East Worcester, Worcester Shenevus, and Maryland, we come to the junction of the Cooperstown and Susquehanna Valley Railroad, for Portlandville, Milford, Clinton, Phœnix, and

COOPERSTOWN.

This pleasant town, which has recently become a place of large resort, was named after Fenimore Cooper, often called the Scott of America. The village is situated on the shore of Otsego, a beautiful lake worthy of being the fountain-head of the bright flowing Susquehanna. Every one who has read the "Deerslayer" or the "Pioneer," knows something of its beauty. Every nook, inlet, cliff, hill, and mountain, contain something of historic interest or living poetry. We subjoin the following passage from the former of these works, as descriptive of the lake and surrounding hills: "On a level with the point lay a broad sheet of water, so placid and limpid that it resembled a *bed of the pure mountain atmosphere* compressed into a setting of hills and woods. At its northern or nearest end it was bounded by an isolated mountain; lower land falling off east and west, gracefully relieving the sweep of the outline; still the character of the country was mountainous; high hills or low mountains rising abruptly from the water on quite nine-tenths of its circuit. But the most striking peculiarity of the scene were its solemn solitude and sweet repose. On all sides, wherever the eye turned, nothing met it but the mirror-like surface of the lake, the placid view of heaven, and the dense setting of woods. So rich and fleecy were the outlines of the forest, that the whole visible earth, from the rounded mountain-top to the water's edge presented one unvaried hue of unbroken verdure." The same points still exist which "Leather Stocking" then saw. There is the same beauty of verdure along the hills, and the sun still glints as brightly as then the ripples of the clear water. There are some things that are constant even upon earth, and surely the unchanging stars should have a changeless mirror! Cooper himself says in the preface, "Even the points exist, a little altered by civilization, but so nearly answering to the description as to be easily recognized by all who are familiar with the scenery of this particular region." Cooperstown is the place to go to read the works of Cooper. For even in reading them we are surrounded by the same inspiration which produced them. The rock near the lake is still pointed out where the tribes were wont to assemble to make treaties and bury the hatchet, and perhaps it will outlast the marble shaft of Cooper's monument surmounted by Leather Stocking and his dog. At least the cellar walls of his mansion are already overgrown, dust to dust, in the last stage of ruin. Mount Vision, a little to the north, overlooks the village, and still further to the north is Prospect Cliff. Like Lake Mahopac, it is literally surrounded by beauty; and like Irvington or Tarrytown, it is one of the literary Meccas of our country. Here, too, are the finest fishing grounds and Otsego is world-wide renowned for its bass and pickerel. The new steamboat christened "Natty Bumppo," capable of accommodating 300 persons, is intended to run three times a day during the season, touching at Three-Mile Point, Five-Mile Point, and Springfield landing, connecting with stages at the head of the lake for Richfield Springs, for Cherry Valley, and Fort Plain—Richfield Springs, seven miles from landing, Cherry Valley eight, and Fort Plain eighteen; also connecting with railroad *en route* to and from these places. There will also be frequent pleasure-trips around the lake. In short, Natty will make *herself* generally interesting and agreeable in the hands of an agreeable captain, A. W. Springstead. There is no place where mountain and lake scenery are better combined.

THE COOPER HOUSE.
The verandahs of the cut are in contemplation.

This hotel is in every particular one of the finest and best-furnished summer resorts in the United States. It stands on the highest ground in the village, 80 feet above the lake, 1,200 feet above the sea, and is surrounded by a fine park of over seven acres, handsomely planted with shade-trees and with Croquet, Ball, and Archery Grounds within the enclosure. The internal arrangements of the house are complete with all the modern improvements, including bells, gas in every room, hot and cold baths, etc. Among the many improvements inaugurated by the present proprietors, Coleman & Maxwell [William B. Coleman, of the

New York Hotel and Albert Maxwell, late Superintendant of the Union Club]. We notice the removal of all the buildings in the rear of the hotel, and the embellishment of the grounds. The watering-places of Richfield and Sharon Springs can be reached by a delightful drive of two or three hours. Cooperstown is within four hours from Albany or Binghamton by rail, and there is communication twice each way daily. Omnibuses will run regularly from the Cooper House to and from the steamer and favorite prospects. In the central part of the village is a fine hotel, styled the Central House, W. C. Keyes & Son, proprietors. It is kept open summer and winter, and justly deserves the fine reputation it has obtained among persons traveling, either on business or pleasure. Returning to the main line of the Albany and Susquehanna, we pass through Colliers and come to Emmons, 79 miles from New York. A stage connects at this point for Delhi and other villages in the Delaware valley. The next station is Oneonta, one of the most stirring villages on our route. Here trains stop fifteen minutes for refreshments. The next station is Otego. Here there is also a stage connection for Franklin, a town doubtless so named as a monument to "Poor Richard." It is pleasant and highly instructive to know that the first child born in town was T. Edgerton. The last one is not yet reported. It is also said that a man by the name of Briggs keeps school there. The village is pleasant, educational, and prosperous. Passing through Wells' Bridge, we come to Unadilla, 99 miles from New York, a town of considerable length, of about 1,000 population. The principal street is finely shaded. At this place unite the Susquehanna and Unadilla rivers. The next place is Sidney, one hundred and three miles from New York, named after Sir Sidney Smith, the British Admiral, by an English schoolmaster then living in Sidney Plains. The next town, Bainbridge, one hundred and eight miles from Albany, incorporated 1825. The first settlement was made in 1785, by settlers from Vermont and Connecticut. Feb. 16, 1791, it took unto itself the name of Jericho. April, 1814, it was changed to its present name. Passing through Afton, with its fine suspension bridge on the left, and Harpersville, we come to the Tunnel, one hundred and twenty-seven miles from New York. In passing through it, we are reminded of the tubular bridge across the Montreal. Its length is about twenty-three hundred feet. Then passing through Osborne Hollow, and Port Crane, we come to

BINGHAMTON

the terminus of our route, one hundred and forty-two miles from Albany, and connecting with Erie railway trains to and from the southern tier counties, and to the west and southwest; also with Delaware, Lackawanna, and Western, and Syracuse and Binghamton railways. This is one of the most enterprising and thorough towns on the Erie Railroad. Population about 16,000. Albany, New York, and Binghamton are, as it were, the three points of an equilateral triangle. The best Hotel is the "Spaulding House," W. F. Spaulding, proprietor, near the Depot, in reference to the excellence of which so much has already been said in our newspapers and public prints that it is almost unnecessary to make the above statement. It is no exaggeration to say that more references have been made in newspapers and periodicals to this Hotel than any other in the country. The rooms are finely decorated and adorned with pictures. Suits of rooms richly furnished are arranged for companies or parties. The surrounding grounds are tastily laid out. In fact *taste* is the word which characterizes everything connected with it. If any one accuses us of being lavish in our praise it will be easy to find confirmation. Go and see! Binghamton has also a widely known Water Cure, a cut of which is given on the next page.

This Institution was established in Binghamton in 1849, since which time it has treated successfully thousands of invalids. The Cure is beautifully situated on the side of Mt. Prospect, surrounded by large trees, and commanding a fine view of the city, rivers, hills, and the magnificent scenery in the immediate vicinity, and abundantly supplied with pure, soft spring water, the *great essentials for hydropathic purposes.*

Dr. and Mrs. O. V. Thayer have the entire charge of the medical department. Their large experience and extensive public and hospital practice for more than twenty years, and the success attending their labors, gives them confidence in recommending their Institution as a place where sick people *can be cured.* Surgical as well as medical cases are solicited. All needful surgical operations skillfully performed, and the hygienic treatment, so successful to rapid recovery, continued at the Cure when necessary.

From the cut below you will get a good idea of the beauty of the location and surroundings. For further particulars address the proprietor, O. V. Thayer. We have now attempted to give in a sketchy way the

BINGHAMTON WATER CURE.

various points of interest from Albany to Binghamton. We are certain that all who have an "eye for scenery" will enjoy the trip, and all who pass a summer among the hills and valleys of the Susquehanna Valley will feel a species of silent gratitude to the Fates for thither directing them.

THE WHITE MOUNTAINS.

Twenty years ago when we studied Peter Parley's Geography, and read the description of the great mountains of New Hampshire, we imagined that they were at least a week's journey from civilization. From that erudite and pleasant work (conducted like Bunyan's master piece in the garb of a Pilgrim), we reached such perfection that we could even give the approximate height of those mountain peaks without looking in the book; but we had no idea how high a mile and a quarter was *perpendicularly up*, and it was not until we walked it on one occasion that we fully realized it. In that age we were deprived of the glowing descriptions of modern Guide-books. No poetry clung to the bare rocks (S. T. 1860. X). No flowers sprung for us by the side of Garnate Pools and Beecher Cascades. To us the White Mountains were continual winter. To paraphrase the eloquent apostrophe of Webster: "The same Heavens are indeed over our heads, the same mountain billows lay at our feet as we look down from glorious Mount Washington, but all else how changed!" Then a few hardy pioneers were *blazing* their way through the mountain passes, and a few adventurers were accomplishing that wonder of wonders the ascent of Mount Washington. Now magnificient Hotels, as pleasant as Roman Villas in the palmy days of the Empire, fill the mountain passes, and gentlemanly proprietors meet the visitor with hearty greetings and smiles as bland as the famous Chinee of poetic memory who long ago ceased to be a Heathen. The cheerful drawing-rooms are filled with visions of beauty as if the German Legend were realized, and the fairies who live in the heart of oak, as well as "heart of poet," were summoned in festive gathering. Oh mystery of Saratoga, Newport and White Mountain *Trunks!* I think the author of fairy legends who imprisoned beauty in the trunks of forest trees was the clear prophet of the gauzy future, and looked with silent awe on lace and ribbons, and airy movables transported and checked by "common carriers." If Peter Parley could come back with his tape measure of mountain heights and take a substantial dinner on the very spot where Crawford *killed the bear*, he would be prepared to add a new chapter on civilization.

Presuming that the tourist is pleasantly located in one of the "mountain villas," we propose in a brief way to point out the places of interest in his immediate neighborhood. If he has arrived by way of the Connecticut River Valley or North Conway, he will probably find himself at the Twin Mountain House, the Crawford or the Profile. If he has arrived *via* Portland and Gorham, we presume he is at the Glen House, or perhaps by either route has reached the summit, enjoying a fine prospect or waiting for the clouds to migrate. The Twin Mountain

A. T. & O. F. BARRON, PROPRIETORS.

This cut gives but an imperfect idea of the Hotel as now completed.

House, only eight miles from Bethlehem, the present terminus of the Boston, Concord and Montreal Railroad, is pleasantly located on the Ammonoosuc River, on a rise of ground which commands a full view of the White and Franconia Ranges. This is, therefore, the nearest mountain house by Railroad approach, and is only ten miles from Mount Washington Depot of the Elevated Railway to the summit. This is the pleasant threshold of mountain travel, and is held in cheerful prospect and pleasing remembrance by the coming and departing tourist.

From this House parties can diverge to all points about the Mountains. Nine miles distant to the Crawford House, the White Mountain Notch and Mount Willard; eleven miles to the Willey House; sixteen to the Profile House; eleven to the Waumbeck House; thirty to the Glen House, *via* "Cherry Mountain Road;" twenty-eight to the Alpine House.

The Crawford House is located in the very heart of the White Mountains, near the entrance of the famous White Mountain Notch, about two thousand feet above the sea. The Willey House is only three miles distant. Passing a little pond the source of the Saco, Elephants Head, the Gateway, the Flume and Silver cascade, we come to the House where on the night of August 28, 1826, the fearful landslide occurred which buried the Willey family. The particulars of this sad tragedy will be found in the "White Hills," by Starr King. You will remember they rushed from the house and were all buried beneath this avalanche of rocks while the deserted house remained unharmed. The Bible was open on the table, and some say at the 16th Psalm.

"The Lord also thundered in the Heavens, and the Highest gave his voice; hailstones and coals of fire. Then the channels of waters were seen, and the foundations of the world were discovered at thy rebuke, O Lord, at the blast of the breath of thy nostrils. He sent from above, he took me, he drew me out of many waters. He brought me forth also into a large place; he delivered me, because he delighted in me."

In the early history of New Hampshire this pass was the great highway to and from Portsmouth, and a turnpike was built at a cost of $40,000. Starr King says, "The first article of commerce that was carried in this way from the sea shore was a barrel of rum. It was taxed heavily in its own substance however to insure its passage, and reached the Ammonoosuc meadows west of the Notch in a very reduced condition." Beecher's Cascade is a short distance in rear of the Crawford House. About five miles north of the Hotel are the Ammonoosuc Falls. This Hotel is also the starting point for the Bridle Path route, and the nearest to White Mountain Railway. Persons preparing to ascend the mountain must look well to their clothing, and be provided with thick gloves, an extra coat, cloak or shawl.

THE SUMMIT OF MOUNT WASHINGTON.

Poetically speaking, Fingal's Cave, on the western coast of Scotland is a *poem* carved in stone; possessing beauty, rythm and symmetry. Mount Washington is a *Chapter of Revelations* lifted above the clouds full of sublimity, solitude and majesty. Amid these wonders and glories of creation we find our own relative *littleness*.

One temple of worship after another crumbles into dust, but the arches and columns of that Ocean temple, which also in perfection rose without the sound of a hammer, and the dome of these mountain peaks whose loose boulders would build a City of Coliseums, eternal in the wreck of time mock the conceited skill of man. There may be places where the Creator's *existence* is equally manifest, but we believe there are none where his truth and power are more legibly "written and lead into the rock forever;" none where we feel more forcibly, "what is man that thou art mindful of him, or the son of man, that thou visitest him."

From Mr. Burt's Connecticut Valley Guide (a comprehensive work which ought to be republished), we subjoin the following description:

"The summit upon which you stand, covering about an acre and a half, is comparatively level, and is made up of a broken mass of dark mica slate, so rough that it is with great difficulty that you walk over it. Here are the Tip Top and Summit Houses, built of the loose rocks, the roofs of which are made secure by long chain cables passing over them and then fastened to the rocks below.

North of the Tip Top House, and a part of the White Mountain range, are Mts. Clay, Jefferson, Adams and Madison.

Easterly, seemingly not far from the base of Mount Washington, is the Androscoggin valley, while in the distance, rising from the central forests of Maine, is Mount Katahdin.

South-east, and directly below you, are Carter and Pinkham Notches, Further beyond are ponds in Maine and the harbor at Portland, the latter 76 miles distant. Lovewell's pond, where an Indian tragedy once occured, can also be seen. Mount Kearsarge also stands prominently before you.

South the sharp peak of Chocorua is seen, touching the very sky, while a little to the right of it is Lake Winnipisoegee. Still beyond the dim outlines of Monadnock are seen.

South-west are Mountains Carrigan and Lafayette.

West lies the beautiful valley of the Ammonoosuc. Beyond are the Green Mountains, Camel's Hump, Mount Mansfield and Jay Peak, standing prominently in the distant view. With favorable light it is claimed that one of the highest peaks of the Adirondacks can been seen.

East of the Tip Top House is Tuckerman's Ravine, named after Prof. Edward Tuckerman, of Amherst College, who used to explore it years ago to complete his knowledge of the lichens and flora of the White Mountain region. The distance from the Tip Top House to the bottom is about a mile. Here, sheltered from the sun, the snow remains nearly through the year, only disappearing in August, a few weeks before it falls again. By the melting of the snow underneath, a beautiful arch is formed, which can be seen usually as late as August. It is a wild and interesting place, and if time will permit it should be visited."

From the summit persons may go down the carriage road to the Glen House on the east side of Mount Washington, or returning for the present via the Elevated Railway or Bridle Path, pay the Franconia scenery a visit in the vicinity of the Profile House. This Hotel is situated on the highest ground in the Franconia Notch, about 2,000 feet above the sea. Like the love-retreat which Claude Melnotte painted so eloquently to the Lady of Lyons, it is shut in by mountain peaks from the rude world. Cannon Mountain on the west, and Eagle Cliff on the east.

PROFILE MOUNTAIN

Is the great object of interest. You get the best view of this elderly gentleman (fastened to the rock after the manner of old Prometheus), early in the morning, or in the early twilight. A walk of about a quarter of a mile down the south carriage road brings one to the best stand point. It is so marked in resemblance that you will not have to call on your imagination, and we recall one of Whittiers' grand descriptions:

> "Like a sun-rimmed cloud
> The great Notch mountains shone,
> Watched over by that solemn browed
> And awful face of stone."

Profile and Echo Lake are also in the immediate neighborhood. This is the best starting point for Mount Lafayette pilgrims, five thousand feet high, which would seem something of a mountain were it not under the wing of Mount Washington. Four and five miles south of the Profile are the Basin and the Pool, worn by the waters of the Pemigewasset; but perhaps the crowning wonder is the Stone Wedge, or Boulder of the Flume. In the words of Starr King:

"Leaving the wagon, we mount by a foot path that leads nearer and nearer to the sweet melody that gives a promise to the ear, which is not to be broken to the hope. Soon we reach the clean and sloping granite floors, over which the water slips in thin, wide, even sheets of crystal colorlessness. Above this, we meet those gentle ripples over rougher ledges that are embossed with green. Then, still higher up, where the rocks grow more uneven, we are held by the profuse beauty of the hues shown upon the bright stones at the bottom of the little translucent basins and pools. Still above, we come to the remarkable fissure in the mountain, more than fifty feet high and several hundred feet long, which narrows too, toward the upper end, till it becomes only twelve feet wide, and which doubtless an earthquake made for the passage of the stream which the visitors are now to ascend. We go up, stepping from rock to rock, now walking along a little plank pathway, now mounting by some rude steps, here and there crossing from side to side of the ravine by primitive little bridges, that bend under the feet and that are railed by birch poles, and then climbing the rocks again, while the spray breaks upon us from the dashing and roaring stream, until we arrive at a little bridge which spans the narrowest part of the ravine. How wild the spot is! which shall we admire most,—the glee of the little torrent that rushes beneath our feet, or the regularity and smoothness of the frowning walls through which it goes foaming out into the sunshine; or the splendor of the dripping emerald mosses; or the trees that overhang their edges; or the huge boulder, egg-shaped, that is lodged between the walls just over the bridge where we stand,—as unpleasant to look at, if the nerves are irresolute, as the sword of Damocles, and yet held by a grasp out of which it will not slip for centuries."

Thus, in brief, we have referred to the principal points of our American Switzerland. The sketch is indeed hasty, but the traveler who consults his own interest will not make a hasty pilgrimage. Do not visit this Mountain region as you would hurry through the streets of Europe, or on the Exchange in Wall street.

Names and heights of the different Mountains:

Mount Washington,	6,285	feet.
" Adams,	5,800	"
" Jefferson,	5,700	"
" Madison,	5,400	"
" Monroe,	5,400	"
" Clay,	5,400	"
" Franklin,	4,900	"
" Pleasant,	4,800	"
" Clinton,	4,200	"
" Jackson,	4,100	"
" Webster,	4,000	"

As the White Mountains were fated to loose their old Indian names (Agiochook, Ammonoosuc, Moosehillock, Cantoocook, Pennacook, and Pentucket,) it is a pity that the party from Lancaster, New Hampshire, who in 1820, appointed themselves godfathers of these mountain peaks could not have afforded Webster one of the highest mountain monuments in the Granite State.

LAKE WINNEPESAUKEE, PLYMOUTH, AND THE WHITE MOUNTAINS, via BOSTON, CONCORD AND MONTREAL AND WHITE MOUNTAINS, N. H., RAILROAD.

J. E. LYON, President. J. A. DODGE, Superintendent.

If a person twenty years ago taking breakfast at Boston had announced to his friends that he intended taking tea that evening on the top of Mount Washington, he would have been considered "a stranger in those parts," or partially insane. And if such person had possessed

the gift of prophecy and dared to announce his vision, that a "ladder of iron" would be lifted through the clouds to the summit of that mountain, safe and secure, with tourists ascending and descending thereon, such prophet would have been reminded of the Tower of

Babel, and the presumptuous builders on the plains of Shinar. But today it creates no surprise to hear our neighbor at the Revere House breakfast-table, telling his friend that he intends taking his supper *the same day* amid the sunset glories of Mount Washington, and probably, if we are in the telegraph office that evening, we may "catch the click" of a voice upon the mountains, and hear that our neighbor is picking his teeth with the highest satisfaction, and a lofty air on the greatest altitude east of the Mississippi. Wonders and miracles do not belong to our generation. Our dreams are made of Hematite ore and nailed to the rocks with iron spikes. The time and toil of years gone by are reduced to a mere fraction by the present conveniences and facilities of travel.

Leaving New York in the evening or Boston 7.30 A.M., the tourist can go thus direct *via* the Boston, Concord and Montreal, or stop over on the route at the various points of interest, which everywhere abound in the lake and mountain district of New Hampshire. The Boston and New York lines unite at Concord 10.30 A.M., and soon after we come in view of that beautiful Lake Winnepesaukee, which, in the estimation of every traveler, finds special favor and obtains the warmest praise. In speaking of the lake scenery, Edward Everett said with no less truth than beauty:

"I have been something of a traveler in our own country, and in Europe have seen most that is attractive, from the Highlands of Scotland to the Golden Horn of Constantinople,—from the summit of the Hartz Mountain to the Fountain of Vaucluse,—but my eye has yet to rest on a lovelier scene than that which smiles around you as you sail from Weirs Landing to Centre Harbor."

At Weirs the new steamer the "Lady of the Lake," connects with the cars taking passengers for Centre Harbor or North Conway, the terminus of the Eastern and Ogdensburgh Railroad. North Conway is everywhere known as one of the loveliest *thresholds* to the White Mountains. In the midst of a gentle meadow scenery and in sight of the mountains, which even in summer seem *whitened* with snow, we can appreciate if anywhere in New England the well-known lines of Moore,

"Whose head in wintry grandeur towers,
And *whitens* with eternal sleet;
While summer in a vale of flowers
Is sleeping rosy at his feet."

The excursions in every direction are charming, and the new hotel the Kiarsarge presents an additional attraction to the many friends of North Conway. Returning to Weirs the next station of importance is

PLYMOUTH,

the charming village where Starr King advises "a day or two's delay mid its meadows and elms." This place is naturally a central point to travelers, and here is located the Pemigewasset House, one of the most

PEMIGEWASSET HOUSE, PLYMOUTH.

spacious and best conducted hotels in New England, C. M. Morse, Manager. It is situated near the confluence of Bakers river, with the Pemigewasset just at the opening of the Franconia and White Mountain ranges, in one of the most picturesque and delightful regions of New Hampshire. Tourists find this a pleasant home for themselves and families while visiting Mount Prospect, Livermore

Falls, Squam Lake, and other places in the neighborhood. And every person who is fortunate enough to touch this Railroad hem of Winnepesaukee's beauty ought at least remain long enough to see with Whittier (in that beautiful word-painting of the Bridal of Pennacook),

> "The sunset with its bars of purple gold,
> *Like a new heaven* shine upward from the lake
> Of Winnepiscogee, and feel
> The sunrise breezes midst the leafy isles
> Which stoop their summer beauty to the lips
> Of the bright waters."

Cars leave morning and noon for Profile, Twin Mountain and Crawford Houses *via* Littleton, Whitefield, Lancaster and Bethlehem; and stages *via* Pemigewasset Valley and Franconia Notch for the various points of interest in the mountain region.

One pleasant feature of this Boston, Concord and Montreal route has already without doubt been noticed by the tourist. Like the Shore Line route from Boston to Portland it is free from dust. It runs up the valleys of the Merrimack, Winnepesaukee, Pemigewasset, Ammonoosuc and Connecticut Rivers, and for thirty miles on the borders of Lake Winnepesaukee, and is not surpassed for its lake and mountain scenery by any road in New England.

By the enterprise of this Company the Railroad has, during the last few years, been pushed into the very heart of the mountains, lessening the fatigue of the mountain trip. Bethlehem is the new terminus of the route, where we arrive at four P.M. The Twin Mountain House is only four miles distant. The White Mountain House eight, and the Crawford thirteen, the Mount Washington Depot only fourteen miles. Those who wish can ascend to the summit and see the mountains in their grandeur, "when they clothe themselves with thick shadows." They will get the supper we promised them at the commencement, and what is still better, "feast upon the sunset glories that crown this monarch of hills six thousand three hundred feet high."

The Mount Washington Railway, above the clouds has been visited by thousands from all parts of the world, and the exhileration awakened by the trip, which takes an hour or more, can only be compared to that of a balloon ascent. New cars and engines, competent employees and a careful management render accidents almost impossible. For six years, since the road was first begun, no workman has been injured, and for the three years that trains have been running, no passenger has been harmed. The powerful ratchet arrangement renders the falling backward of the car as impossible as the winding backward of one's watch. In going down, the atmospheric brakes are added to common friction brakes, so that a stop is made instantly, at pleasure. The progress up and down is made at the rate of a moderate walk, so that the ever changing landscape is enjoyed at leisure. Most of people have hitherto reached the summit at noon, when a vertical light gives but a tame idea of the surroundings as seen by sunset and sunrise. Ample accommodations are made for guests on the mountain.

And now we leave you among these mountains to pursue your journey as pleasure calls; to Lake Memphremagog, Montreal, Quebec, the Saguenay, Niagara Falls, Lake George, Saratoga, the Green Mountains, Portland and the sea side—from Hampton Beach to Newport and Long Branch.

MEMPHREMAGOG HOUSE.

THE GREEN MOUNTAINS.

If any section of our country is appropriately named, that section is *Vermont*. Very few of the original thirteen States, and the later twenty-three, or the "daughters of the wilderness" pining for the Union, have names which mean anything in particular. Like Mr. Weller's initial, most of the names have depended " wery much on the

taste of the *speller*." A few carry with them a fragment of history, an Indian tradition, or a morsel of royal flattery. (Virginia, in memory of the Virgin Queen. Pennsylvania, in memory of a generous-hearted man. New York, in memory of the white rose of a triumphant house after the long struggles of York and Lancaster. Maryland, Louisiana, Carolina, also of individual interest. Massachusetts, Connecticut, Alabama, &c., of Indian origin). It was reserved for almost the extreme Northern and Southern State, Florida, the land of flowers, and Vermont, the land of mountains, to *syllable* their condensed characteristics; no one will ever need to consult history to appreciate their significance; and as Florida year by year becomes more and more the tendency of winter resort, so more and more Vermont calls the summer tourist to her beautiful valleys, clear streams and mountain shadows. From end to end extends a chain of mountains. Like a furrow turned up by the Titans, or a burial mound of giants, this immense ridge of green (from two to five thousand feet high) slopes on the west to the blue waters of Champlain, and and on the east to the fertile valley of the Connecticut. We propose in this hasty sketch to speak in the order following of Manchester, Poultney, Middletown, Brattleboro, Bellow's Falls, Stowe and Alburgh Springs.

MANCHESTER.

The routes are from New York *via* Harlem and Harlem Extension Railroads, or *via* Hudson River Railroad, and from Troy *via* Troy and Boston Railroad. From Saratoga *via* Troy, and also *via* Rutland. From Boston *via* Fitchburg, Bellows Falls and Rutland, or *via* Boston and Albany Railroads to Chatham Four Corners, thence by Harlem Extension to Manchester. From Rutland *via* Harlem Extension Railroad. From Burlington *via* Rutland and Harlem Extension.

From St. Albans, Missisquoi Springs, Highgate Springs, Montpelier, Stowe, Newport, Plattsburg, and all points North, by Vermont Central Railroad or Steamers to Burlington, thence by Railroad to Manchester.

From Middletown Springs, Clarendon Springs, White Mountains, Lake George, &c., by Railroad from Rutland to Manchester.

From St. Louis, Chicago, Niagara Falls, and all points West, by N. Y. Central Railroad to Troy,—Troy and Boston and Harlem Extension Railroads to Manchester.

This village is nicely shaded, and has the finest promenades conceivable, being paved with slabs of white marble from the neighboring quarries. On Main street are situated the bank, the Congregational church, the court-house, post-office, and, centrally located, the

"Equinox House," Mr. F. H. Orvis, proprietor, in the immediate vicinity of which are the telegraph and the office of the *Manchester Journal*. It is published by D. K. Simonds, Proprietor, and is one of the most reliable local newspapers in the State. The Episcopal church is nearly completed, and the Congregational Building is in every particular a success. There is also a flourishing Masonic Lodge and a Chapter (the Adoniram F. & A. M.) The "Music Hall," erected two years ago by the proprietor of the Equinox House, is the finest building of the kind in Vermont, and here are enjoyed concerts, tableaux, theatricals, readings, both private and public.

THE EQUINOX HOUSE.

The Equinox House is one of the most successful hotels in our country; and this success is not only due to location, but also to the cleanliness of every thing connected with it, and its liberally supplied table. Every thing from billiards to fine drives, from bowling-alleys to fine scenery, from trout fishing to marble quarries, from mountain wildness to marble pavements, Manchester possesses. Those who love trout fishing will find no finer spot to spend the summer; and Mr. Charles Orvis, of Manchester, will save the trouble of bringing rod and line, as he keeps everything needed for the descendants of Isaac Walton. The roads are excellent, and pedestrians will find no difficulty in ascending the loftiest peaks, which abound with wild and picturesque glens, made familiar by the pencils of Durand, Boughton, Tyler, and Boutelle. From the summit of Mount Equinox we see, in the southeast, Greylock and the Stratton mountains; on the east, Grand Monadnock and Ascutney peak. To the northeast rise the peaks of Killington and Shrewsbury; and far away the

BURR AND BURTON SEMINARY.

summits of the Kearsarge and Franconia mountains. To the southwest we have a full view of the distant Catskills. On bright days Lakes George and Champlain may be seen to the northwest, and the villages of Saratoga Valley. One may learn a lesson from these mountain peaks. We see below us a map not bounded by crooked lines which mark the States, and counties, and townships, but a map reaching out, as it were, one and indivisible, bound together by every brook and rivulet, and clasped and riveted by chains of eternal hills.

Right below us stands the "Burr and Burton Seminary," with its grand outlook upon village, and valley, and mountain—a location not surpassed by that of any educational institution in the land.

Here such men as Dr. Coleman, Dr. Worcester, Dr. Wickham, and Professors Stoddard, Albee, and Burnham, have done more and better work fitting young men for college, than has been done at any other school in Vermont. A few years ago a department of young ladies was added to the Seminary, and now youth of both sexes may there get an excellent English or classical education. The Principal, Rev. L. A. Austin, A. M., devotes himself to the collegiate-preparatory department, and we can warrant that any boy with brains, who goes through his rigid three years' course, will be thoroughly fitted to take and maintain a high standing in any of our colleges. The Principal has earnest professional teachers associated with him in all departments. The special advantages of the school are, its beautiful and healthful location, the favorable moral influences surrounding it, its limited number of boarding pupils (40), constituting with the teachers a family, its strict discipline, its thorough instruction, and the low rates for board and tuition. It has also funds enabling it to give generous aid to deserving pupils who need help.

It is in all respects a good place for good pupils. If bad ones come, they must reform under its strict but kindly discipline, or be speedily dismissed.

Here also, centrally located in Manchester, is the Vanderlip House, a Hotel which has enjoyed for more than a quarter of a century the reputation of a first class and home-like Hotel. The rooms are high and airy, dining-rooms large and pleasant, and the parlor some sixty feet by forty. One hundred boarders can be easily accommodated. The grounds are nicely shaded, and from the windows there is a fine view of the mountains. Manchester is certainly one of the pleasantest places in which to spend a summer. All the citizens seem bound together for the common interest. They appreciate the fact that they have a pleasant place for a Summer Resort, a *fact* which is continually spreading, until now the sunset shadows of the grand old Equinox cover a good portion of New York and Philadelphia. The Elm House is also pleasantly located, and has undergone during the year thorough and extensive repairs. Nor ought we forget the rural cemetery of Manchester, appropriately named

"Dellwood." The land for it was given by Judge Skinner, of Chicago, son of the late Governor Skinner, of Vermont, who resided in Manchester. By the efforts of Mr. A. G. Clark, President of the Association, it is being made one of the prettiest cemeteries in the country. There is a fine Green House connected with it, and the grounds are finely laid out in walks and drives. The monuments erected show the taste of Mr. Fullerton, in whose shop, near the depot of Manchester, we saw some work which would adorn the cemetery of Greenwood, and, indeed, some

VANDERLIP HOUSE.

of the monuments in Greenwood are of his design and finish. From a rustic monument with its vines and leaves to the finished arch and column, everything is complete. When last there he was finishing a monument for Mayor Brackett of Rochester. Resting on a granite and marble base four columns of Vermont Italian marble supports a canopy after the manner of the gothic monument to Walter Scott in Edinburgh. Another quite similar was also being made for Samuel Hallett of Wayne. The cost of these are $5,000. All persons who visit Manchester will be well repaid in looking over the work and workshop at the depot,

POULTNEY AND MIDDLETOWN.

The village of Poultney is sixty-seven miles north of Troy, on the Rutland and Washington division of the Rensselaer and Saratoga Railroad. It is one of the finest villages in the western Vermont valley. Here is located the Ripley College known as the Vermont Summer Home.

The building is of brick, situated eighteen rods back from the street, surrounded by ten acres of lawn and grove. There are no other buildings nearer than twenty rods; it has an unobstructed circulation of fresh air, and is entirely excluded from the noise and dust of the street. It is only eighty rods from the Poultney station of the Rutland and Washington Railroad. No locality has in the same compass a greater number of charming drives, in the midst of picturesque and beautiful scenery, than Poultney. The mineral springs of Middletown, which are already known in almost every city, town, and village of our country, are only eight miles distant by an excellent road which follows the Poultney River, winding through the mountains and presenting to the traveler a succession of ever-varying landscape. Lake Bomoseen and St. Catherine, the former nine and the latter six miles long, are also within easy drives. It is also a matter of interest to know that this is the place where Horace Greeley says he learned what he knows of the art of printing.

MIDDLETOWN SPRINGS.

The Middletown Springs are situated on the Poultney River, a small stream tributary to Lake Champlain, in Rutland County, Vermont. During the last three years the fame of the Middletown Spring Waters has spread so rapidly that every one is anxious to know where "Middletown" is, and what are its surroundings. These waters have wrought so many triumphs over disease, that the last two summers have brought crowds to these Springs, although there was by no means a hotel of suitable accommodation. Now the wants of the public are satisfied. A magnificent and commodious hotel has been erected, and has been christened by the beautiful name "Montvert." The village, nestled

MONTVERT HOTEL, Middletown Springs, Vt.

among the green hills of Vermont, with its healing waters, pure atmosphere and cool nights, is famous as a quiet, healthful, summer resort, and a most desirable place of rest and recreation for the invalid and pleasure-seeker. The surrounding mountains, hills, valleys, and groves are as full of the genii of health as ever a fairy fountain or grove of the genii of beauty. The drives in every direction are unsurpassed. Take, for instance, the one from Poultney to Middletown. The road follows, most of the way, a stream which winds, now through meadowland, and now dashes through rocks and narrow channels. The road rises to the east, and we will never forget the beautiful sunset we once saw returning to Poultney from the springs. We present here a fine cut of the Montvert. The furnishings of the house are all new. The rooms and hallways, spacious, cheerful, and well ventilated, embracing pleasant apartments for about three hundred guests. The building is lighted throughout with gas. The Springs near the hotel have grown rapidly in popular favor, and these, together with the fine hotel, will insure the success of "Middletown."

BRATTLEBORO.

This village on the eastern side of the Green Mountains, and on the western bank of the Connecticut River, is unrivalled in its reputation as a summer resort. Thousands of visitors from all parts of the country add their testimony to the Southern Switzerland of Vermont. The village is built on four terraces rising from the Connecticut, and on the opposite side rises the mountain wall of Wantastiquiet. The drives are fine in every direction, and no one will half appreciate the beauty of the town and its surroundings without driving at least three or four days, to the prominent points of interest. The Brooks house, a very fine hotel, built at the cost of $150,000, is situated at the corner of Main and High streets, but five hours by rail from Boston, and seven from New York. The parlors, dining-rooms and sleeping apartments, are all spacious and handsomely furnished. Many of the rooms command a fine view of mountain and river. This makes a pleasant half-way house on the route between Boston and the White Mountains.

The Revere house a short distance from the Depot, centrally located, has long enjoyed the reputation of one of the pleasantest hotels in the Connecticut River Valley. Mr. H. C. Nash, owner and proprietor. The business activity of the town is greatly indebted to J. Estey & Co's., Cottage Organ Manufactory—universally recognized as the best manufactured in our country. Two miles west is the pleasant little village of West Brattleboro, and here is located a Ladies' Seminary, whose very name Glenwood is suggestive of classic rest and intellectual quiet.

BROOKS HOUSE, BRATTLEBORO.

ALLEN & BODWELL, PROPRIETORS, ALSO OF STEVENS' HOUSE, NEW YORK.

A place where every breeze breathes health, and every sound is but the echo of tranquility. Its grounds are spacious and so ornamented as to render them peculiarly attractive.

The instruction is given by a full board of teachers, thorough and efficient in all its departments. The preceptress and many of the teachers are especially qualified by years of study and foreign travel In one sentence, everything is finished, nothing superficial, a pleasant home under kind and Christian management. It is also open from the middle of June to the middle of September for summer boarders.

GLENWOOD LADIES SEMINARY, WEST BRATTLEBORO, VT.

BELLOWS FALLS,

220 miles from New York, 225 from Montreal, 101 from White Mountains, 145 from Lake Memphremagog. Across the river was, what was once known as Fall Mountain, about 800 feet high.

In 1856 President Hitchcock, and the students of Amherst and Middlebury, met here and christened it Mount Kilburn, in honor of the hero who fought the Indians so bravely from his little fort below the south end of the mountain. Bellows Falls received its name from Colonel Bellows. The river here descends forty-four feet in half a mile. The windows and wide verandas of the "Island House," a cut of which is here

F. C. FLEMING, (formerly Conductor Conn. River R. R.,) PROPRIETOR.

given, command a fine view of the rapids and surrounding mountains. Tourists will find it a pleasant place. Here were great fishing-grounds among the Indians. Passengers *en route* for Rutland take the Rutland Railroad; northern passengers, the Vermont Central. Passing north through South Charlestown, Charlestown, North Charlestown, and Claremont, and we come to Windsor, lying under the base of the grand old Ascutney

Peak. The height of Mount Ascutney is three thousand three hundred and twenty feet above the level of the sea, and about three thousand feet above the level of the Connecticut River, at Windsor. The village consists mostly of one fine street, nicely shaded. The post-office building is probably the best in Vermont. In the finest part of the street is the Windsor House, a cut of which is here given. The house has justly gained a fine reputation in the hands of Colonel Simonds, whose natural qualifications, together with years of experience, make him one of the

WINDSOR HOUSE.

best landlords on our route. Stop over at Windsor and climb up the old Ascutney. Stop at the Windsor House, walk a few times through the shady streets, have a talk with M. K. Paine, whose reputation has already reached every State in the Union, and then, and *not till then,* go your way rejoicing.

Passing through Hartland, North Hartland, and we come to White River Junction. Passengers for the north, White Mountains, or Lake Memphremagog, at this point take the Passumpsic Railroad. Passengers for Montpelier, Montreal, etc., keep the Vermont Central. Passing through White River village, Woodstock, West Hartford, we come to Sharon, thirteen miles from White River Junction. Passing on through South Royalton, Royalton, Bethel, Randolph, with its pleasant "Cottage Hotel," Braintree, Roxbury, and Northfield, whose glory departed with its machine works to St. Albans, we come to Montpelier, 104 miles from Bellows Falls. This is the capital of Vermont, almost completely sur-

VIEW OF WINDSOR AND ASCUTNEY MOUNTAIN. THE ABOVE CUT WAS ENTERED ACCORDING TO ACT OF CONGRESS IN 1868, BY M. K. PAINE, IN THE CLERK'S OFFICE OF THE DISTRICT COURT OF THE DISTRICT OF VERMONT.

rounded by hills. It was settled in 1786. Became seat of government in 1805. The Onion River (now called the Winooski) and the Worcester branch meet at this place. There are fine drives in almost every direction: along Dog River to Northfield ten miles of level road, and varied scenery; up the Winooski seven miles to Barre, and down the river, twelve miles to Waterbury. The best hotel is "The Pavilion," centrally located on the broad, shady street of the village; near it is the capitol building, a model of architectural taste.

Passing through Middlesex we come to Waterbury, where persons take the stage to one of the largest and most complete summer hotels in the State.

STOWE AND MOUNT MANSFIELD.

The ride from Waterbury to Stowe is pronounced charming by every one, and forms a fine preface to the book of Landscape Beauty which we are about to open. In the distance we see old Mansfield, with Nose and Chin rising above the other mountains, that silent sentinel of the State which looks upon every county from Franklin to Bennington, and counts the stars as they pass in "nightly journey" from the White Mountains to the Adirondacks. Under this mountain, and only eight miles from the summit, is situated the charming country village of Stowe—and here is the famous mount Mansfield Hotel, under the suc-

MOUNT MANSFIELD HOTEL.

cessful management of N. P. Keeler. This new hotel has rooms for four hundred guests. They are large and cheerful, and in suits or private parlors, as may be desired. An extensive livery is connected with the hotel and abundant stable room for those who desire their own teams. Also billiard tables, bowling alleys, cafe, croquet grounds and theatre. Telegraph office near the hotel. A carriage road has been constructed to the summit of Mount Mansfield (about five thousand feet high), on which is an excellent hotel, making the most delightful mountain trip possible.

The walks and drives cannot be surpassed. Sunset Hill, a short distance from the hotel, commands a fine view of the mountains and surrounding country. The drives are fine—Mount Mansfield, eight miles; Smuggler's Notch, one of the most wild and romantic places in the country, eight miles; Bingham's Falls, five miles; Moss Glen Falls, three and one-half miles; Gold Brook, three miles; West Hill, two miles; Morrisville Falls, eight miles; Johnson's Falls, twelve miles; Nebraska, six miles.

The proprietors wish also to state that board will be at a reduced price in harmony with the downward tendency of values, and are determined not to be excelled in attention and courtesy to guests. The Summit House on the top of Mount Mansfield can accommodate about one hundred. From this highest mountain peak of Vermont the eye ranges over a wide extent of country; to the north the valley of the St. Lawrence, and west the Champlain, with the rival mountains of New York, Marcy and Seward, to the south, Camel's Hump, Killington Peak and the grand old Ascutney overlooking Windsor and the valley of the Connecticut, and sixty miles to the east the White and Franconia mountains. If enthusiasm is ever pardoned, the view from this mountain may well speak its apology.

Taking the cars again at Waterbury, twenty-three miles bring us to Essex Junction. Burlington, a beautiful town overlooking the lake is eight miles south from this point, and St. Albans, with its splendid hotel, the Welden House, is twenty-four miles north. Branching from this point are several springs of the finest reputation, the Shelden, Highgate and Missisquoi; and chief among these the Alburgh Spring, with its new and pleasant hotel. They are situated on the railroad to Rouses' Point, seventeen miles from St. Albans. The hotel is on the banks of the beautiful Missisquoi Bay, at the western extremity of Lake Champlain. Here are fine views of lake and highlands and quiet village life, with facilities for boating, shooting and fishing, and the famous springs are themselves fountains of health and strength.

ALBURGH SPRINGS HOUSE,

AT ALBURGH SPRINGS, GRAND ISLE CO., VERMONT,

Sixteen miles North of St. Albans, on the line of the Vermont Central Railroad.

WILLARD SEARS, Proprietor. WM. M. FLETCHER, Manager.

WM. F. SLOCUM, Jr., Clerk.

Post-office Address, Alburgh Springs, Vermont.

This house, on the banks of the beautiful MISSISQUOI BAY, at the northern extremity of Lake Champlain, is one mile from the Railroad. Those who are seeking health and a quiet resort for the summer, will find here combined attractions, at once varied and unique. Mountain air, fine views of lake and highlands, and quiet village life, scenery both picturesque and grand, with facilities for **Boating, Shooting,** and **Fishing,** all add their healthful influences to recuperate the weary dweller and worker in the city; while the famous Alburgh Spring—itself a fountain of health and strength—is inclosed in the grounds of the hotel. For nearly a century this Spring has been the resort of invalids, and some of those healed by it forty years ago, regularly visit it every year. For all diseases of the skin or internal organs, arising from impurity of blood, or deficient nervous power, the water has proved a reliable remedy.

Internal Tumors, Calculi, etc., hopeless cases of Humors, Chronic Rheumatism, Liver and Kidney Complaints, Scrofula, Dyspepsia, Catarrh, etc., etc.,

have yielded to it; and many persons, given over by skillful physicians, have here found, in NATURE'S OWN REMEDY, relief from suffering, and restoration to strength.

To these great natural advantages, the **Alburgh Springs House** adds the comforts of a good Hotel, elegantly furnished, and the quiet of a country home. Guests will be received after May 1st.

VERMONT SUMMER HOME,
RIPLEY COLLEGE, POULTNEY, VERMONT.

Rev. J. NEWMAN, D. D., Proprietor.

Gentlemen living in cities on the Sea Coast, Lakes and Rivers, and desirous of placing their families in the country for the summer, will find it advantageous to inform themselves in regard to this part of Vermont, and particularly in regard to the inducements offered by

Ripley College as a Summer Home.

The Proprietor does not claim that either his house or its management is perfect, nor that *everything* in this region is superior to its like in every other region. He *does*, however, claim that the LOCATION, the HOUSE, and its MANAGEMENT, combine more of the elements of substantial comfort and of a true *Home* than can be found at any other Summer Resort; and that they are offered for less money than will procure them at any other place. For *families* of women and children it is unequaled. For *invalids* it is equal to the best Remedial Institution. Its hundreds of former guests will all testify that, while not alluring as a *fashionable* Resort—as a *Home* it is unsurpassed. The table is always supplied with vegetables and milk from the farm and dairy of the Proprietor, and with the best butter that Vermont can produce. All domestic appointments and arrangements are such as to inspire among guests the feeling that they are in an eminent degree members of one family, rather than mere boarders at a hotel, not interested in each other. The House is of brick, and is disconnected from other Buildings, so as to have free circulation of pure air and be as cool as any house possibly can be. It is retired 18 rods from any street, and is, consequently, as quiet as the inmates please to have it. It is furnished throughout with reference to neatness and comfort. The Rooms are larger than usual in Hotels at Watering places, and are *perfectly* ventilated. The windows all have inside Blinds. The Corridors and Stairways are all carpeted—in short, nothing is lacking which comfort requires, or which the prices asked warrant guests to expect.

Water from the Middletown Springs, distant eight miles, furnished to guests without charge.

THE CONNECTICUT VALLEY.

"Thou lovely vale of sweetest stream that flows,
Winding and willow-fringed Connecticut."

To the White Mountains, Lake Memphremagog, Montreal and Quebec.

Two routes open from New York to the Connecticut Valley, one by the New York and New Haven Railroad, the other by boat to New Haven *via* the *Continental* and *Elm City*, leaving pier No. 25 East River daily at 3.15 P.M. and 11 P.M. The New York and New Haven Railroad was opened for travel January 1849, the double track completed 1854. The thriving villages along the route are conclusive testimony of thorough management, rapid and pleasant transit. They might be considered the *threaded* suburbs of the great metropolis. The Continental and Elm City ply direct between New York and New Haven. Persons taking the 11 P.M. boat connect at New Haven with the morning train up the Connecticut Valley. Persons taking 3.15 P.M. arrive at New Haven 8 P.M., *securing* what every person ought to have at least once a summer, a daylight passage up the Sound. In fact, there can be no finer, cheaper, and quicker excursion for those who have no time for extended travel than the afternoon boat to New Haven. With three hours in the "City of Elms," and returning from New Haven by the 11 P.M. boat, arrive in New York early in the morning. One hundred and fifty miles of invigoration between three in the afternoon and five in the morning.

As we will give hereafter a description of New Haven in our route from New York to Newport, Boston, &c., we will start at once on our northern journey. Taking the New Haven, Hartford and Springfield Railroad, we pass through North Haven, Wallingford and Yalesville to Meriden, a place of rapid growth, manufactories and enterprise. Near the depot is the building of the Meriden Britannia Company, almost five hundred feet in length. The next station to the north is Berlin with two branch Railroads; one to New Britain, two and a half miles to the northwest, the other to Middletown, ten miles to the southeast. Passing through Newington we come to the enterprising and pleasant city of Hartford. Probably more money is *centered* in Hartford than any city of twice its size in the United States. The Insurance Companies, both life and fire have been the most successful in our country. On the right as we come into the depot, we see the block of the Travelers' Insurance Company. There are many fine buildings in Hartford both private and public.

The Retreat for the Insane founded in 1822; the Asylum for the Deaf and Dumb; Wadsworth Atheneum, and, we believe, the State House, of Doric architecture, is also generally included. Colt's manu-

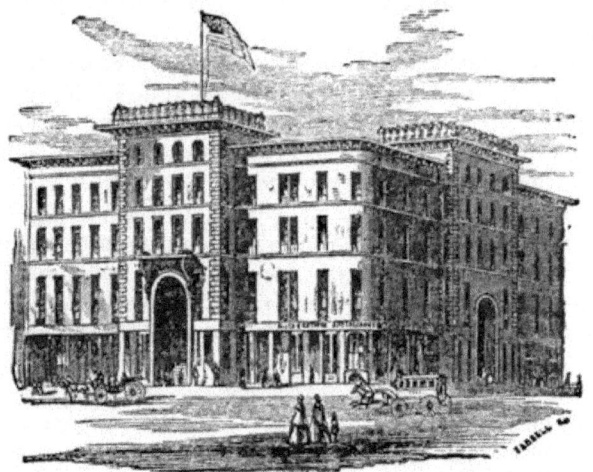

THE ALLYN HOUSE.

factory is extensive. The city was incorporated 1784, the same year with Middletown and New Haven. The Allyn House, situated on the corner of Asylum and Trumbull streets, is first-class in every respect, a cut of which is here given, R. J. Allyn, proprietor. The United States, D. A. Rood, proprietor, is also one of the most popular houses in New England and the largest in Connecticut. Passing through Windsor, the first English settlement in the State, 1633, and birth-place of Roger Wolcott, signer of the Declaration of Independence, Jonathan

Edwards of stern faith, and Oliver Ellsworth, Chief Justice of the United States; Windsor Locks, with its manufactories; Warehouse Point, with its iron truss bridge, over 1,500 feet long; Enfield, on the east, with its large Shaker community, about six miles from the river; Thompsonville, with its immense carpet factories, and Longmeadow, in the edge of Massachusetts, and four miles bring us to

SPRINGFIELD,

the great Railroad centre of New England, and the oldest Massachusetts town in the Connecticut River Valley, settled 1636 by a colony from Roxbury. The Indian name of the town was Agawam; took the name of Springfield, 1840; made a city, 1852. The United States Armory, established here in 1795, has probably done more toward building the city than any other one cause. The grounds, about twenty acres, occupy a large plateau, and are surrounded by an iron fence eight feet high. The building of greatest interest to the visitor is Arsenal Building. It contains 300,000 guns. The first two lines of Longfellow's poem present the briefest description:—

> "This is the arsenal—from floor to ceiling,
> Like a *huge organ*, rise the burnished arms!"

The view from the observatory of the arsenal commands a wide extent of the valley, dotted with villages and manufactories, for Springfield is the centre of a large manufacturing interest.

Thackeray, Jenny Lind and Dickens, considered this view one of the finest in the country. The drives are pleasant in every direction, the streets well shaded, and many elegant residences.

One of the great attractions, however, of Springfield, is the number and extent of its hotels. No city of equal size in the country, can boast of such hotel accomodations. And Springfield owes quite as much to their excellence, as to its great variety of other attractions for the visitor. The two principal Houses, are the "Massasoit" at the station, and "Haynes New Hotel," down town.

Of the "Massasoit," the traveling public for twenty-five years, have fully realized its value and popularity, while the "Haynes House," although comparatively new, has obtained a success, and deserved popularity, almost unprecedented. Its location, a short distance from the station, avoids the smoke and confusion, and is therefore quiet and pleasant for those desiring to make a few days sojourn in this "Heart of the Connecticut valley."

Here also are the offices of the large Paper Manufacturers and dealers. The Union Paper Manufacture Co. Massasoit Paper Manufacturing Co. Bay State Co. Powers Paper Company, &c. Here also is Peck & Bakers large Manufactory of the finest Baby Carriages in the world. So you see Springfield not only supplies our country with

MASSASOIT HOUSE.
Passengers on Through Trains have ample time for Dinner and Supper.
M. & E. S. CHAPIN, Proprietors.

arms, but also our children in arms, better than any town in the Republic. (This joke being rather *apparent* is only intended for heads of families). One more firm also demands our attention, the well-known establishment of Milton Bradley & Co., for what family of children from five to fifty years of age has not known and enjoyed the productions and publications of Milton Bradley & Co., which have done more to keep the young folks of the land at home, by furnishing to their homes the necessary means to render them pleasant and happy, than many sermons on human depravity or the sinfulness of amusements.

The manufactory of this enterprising firm consists of a large brick

building five stories high, with floor area of about twenty-five thousand square feet. The basement floor is devoted to the wood-working machinery, for the manufacture of the popular croquet sets patented by Mr. Bradley, the new game of Magic Hoops, the Kindergarten Alphabet and Builder's Blocks, and numerous parts of other articles. The second floor is occupied by the offices sample-rooms, packing and shipping rooms, etc.

On the third floor the designers and artists have comfortable quarters, also the lithographic printing department, by means of which the beautiful colored pictures are made that are embraced in the various dissected puzzles and games. The upper floors are devoted to the manufacture of the numerous games, puzzles and amusements by which this firm has gained the reputation of elevating the standard of these publications, until they are considered an indispensable part of the stock of every first-class dealer in these goods.

Messrs. Bradley & Co., claim that their establishment is the only one in the country devoted exclusively to the manufacture of their class of goods, and the only one in which all of the various kinds of work are performed by the same firm. Many of the best cuts in our book were made by this firm, and we are pleased to acknowledge their excellence.

Going north from Springfield we take the

CONNECTICUT RIVER RAILROAD.

J. MULLIGAN, Superintendent.

We are now fairly in the Connecticut Valley, and we believe the tourist will have occasion many times to acknowledge the truth of the lines of Holland with which we commence this sketch.

> "Thou lovely vale of sweetest stream that flows,
> Winding and willow-fringed Connecticut."

The Connecticut "Quonechticut" interpreted Long River, or as some say, "without end," rises in the Highlands between the United States and Canada, 1,500 feet above the level of the sea. In the first part of its course it has a rapid fall of 1,200 feet from its source to the mouth of the Passumpsic. From that point it descends 100 feet to the flat bottom, between Windsor and Bellows Falls, Vermont. Thence 160 feet to Deerfield. From Springfield to the Sound 40 feet. Its breadth through Connecticut varies from 100 rods to one half mile; near its mouth it is little more than a mile. The principal streams which flow into it from the west are the Passumpsic at the foot of Fifteen Mile Falls, the White River, the Deerfield, the Westfield, and the Farmington in Connecticut. On the east the Ammonoosuc, Millers, and Chicopee rivers. The valley is about 300 miles long, with a mean breadth of 40 miles.

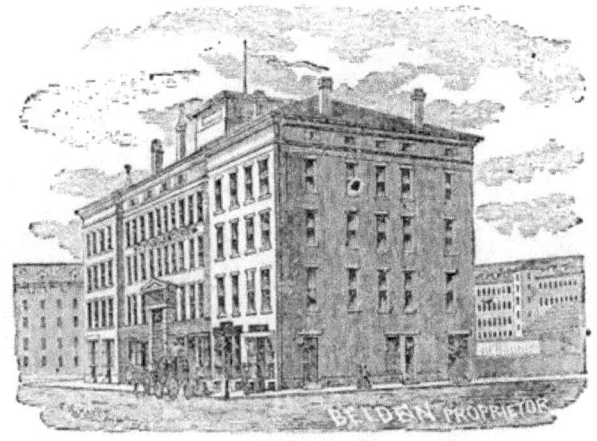

HOLYOKE HOUSE,

E. M. BELDEN, PROPRIETOR, late of the Chicopee House, Chicpee, Mass.

With this description we will once more resume our journey. Passing through Chicopee and Willimansett, we come to Holyoke the "bricky" town of the Connecticut—block after block all brick from garret to basement. This is probably the finest waterpower in the world. Two and a half miles from Holyoke, is situated quiet and beautiful Ingleside, one of the pleasantest drives, likewise from Chicopee and Springfield. Passing north from Holyoke we come to

Smith's Ferry, a little south of Mount Tom. Across the river rises Mount Holyoke, and a few miles bring us to Northampton, "Queen village of the Meads." This is the poetic district of Hollands Kathrina, and on every side has a beautiful horizon. The Mansion House is situated on a fine eminence in the central part of the village, and commands an extensive view. From the observatory we see to the north,

THE MANSION HOUSE, DANIEL P. KINGSLEY.

part of Sugar Loaf and the Deerfield Mountains; to the east the unfenced meadow lands of Hadley and distant Amherst; to the southeast Holyoke and Nonatuck, the terminus of Mount Tom, and the river lies at our feet,

> "Pouring from the north
> Its tumbling tide, and winding down the vale
> Till doubling in a serpent coil, it pauses
> Before the chasm that parts the frontal spurs
> Of Tom and Holyoke."

The house has been thoroughly refitted. The rooms are large and airy, spacious halls and verandahs and cold spring water fountain playing in the halls; coaches and hacks at the depot on the arrival of each train. The Fitch House between the Mansion House and the Depot is a fine brick block recently built, and has already won a wide reputation in this valley of hotels.

FITCH BROTHERS & SIMONDS.

These two hotels so finely conducted form a pleasant brotherhood to those of Springfield.

Northampton was called Nonatuck by the Indians, and purchased from them in 1653. Purchase price as follows :—one hundred fathoms of wampum, ten coats, some smaller gifts, and plowing sixteen acres of land on opposite side of river. (In the purchase of Springfield they stipulated for eighteen fathoms of wampum, eighteen coats, ten hatchets, eighteen hoes, and eighteen knives). Here lies buried David Brainard, the missionary to the Stockbridge Indians. We are now 17 miles from Springfield, 153 from New York, 293 from Montreal, 167 from White Mountains, 212 from Lake Memphremagog, 385 from Quebec.

About two miles west from this pleasant village, and connected by horse railway cars, is situated the historic and poetic "Florence," the main-spring or back-bone of which is the world-renowned Florence Sewing Machine Company. We can judge something of the extent of the rapidly increasing business of this Company from the extent of their manufactory, the main buildings are about 350 feet long, a very correct view of which is here pictured.

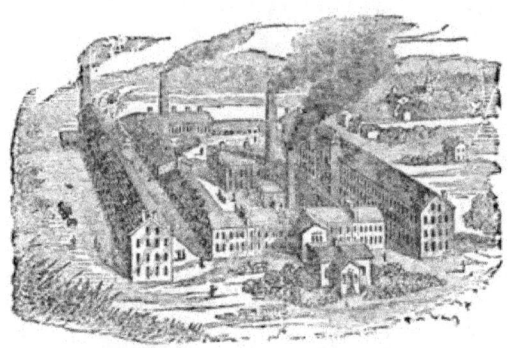

The most complete facilities for the production of everything required to make a perfect sewing machine can be seen here, from the foundry to the most elaborate and highly-finished wood work of the cases, and from the fact that over 300 hands are employed, with a pay-roll of about $25,000 a month. It will well repay one to visit Florence, and pass through the various departments, and trace the various pieces as they pass through the hands of their skilful workmen, until it becomes *in fact* "a thing of beauty." The machine is entirely different from anything else in the market, and its excellencies are appreciated not only in our own country, but in England and the Continent. Some time ago in London, just off from Lombard Street, we saw a large crowd gathered, and thought of course it was some new bulletin from France, when lo! it was the picture of a lady blooming with health, life-size, using a "Florence Sewing machine," and we thought there was no more need of singing, either in London or anywhere, the sad "Song of the Shirt." And also thought of our "Florence," just west of Northampton.

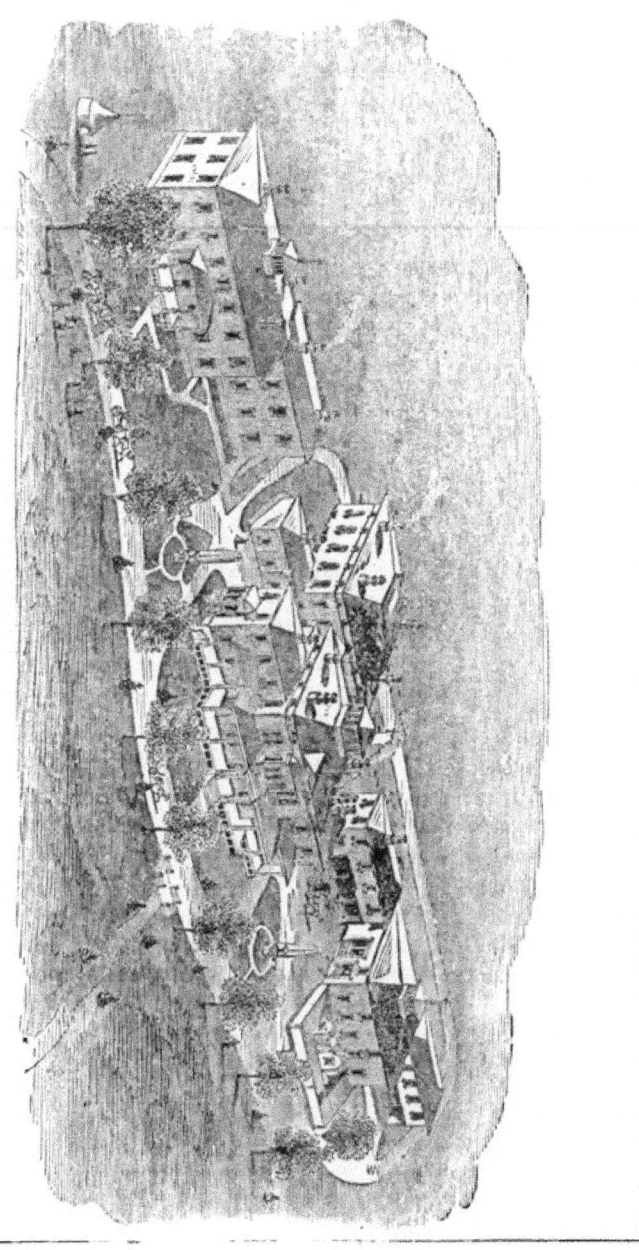
BIRDS-EYE VIEW OF INGLESIDE, HOLYOKE, MASS.

Passing through Hatfield, Whately and South Deerfield we come to Deerfield, a pleasant village, with its long, quiet, shady street. The Pocumtuck Hotel, a cut of which we give on the opposite page, is a pleasant place alike for summer guests or business travelers. In the wide hall of the hotel, in a glass-case (to guard against the penknives of modern kinght-errants), is a door bearing the marks of the tomahawk. It is of yellow pine and closely studded with nails. It suggests Whittier's lines:—

> "Then smote the Indian tomahawk
> On crashing door and shattering lock;
> Then rang the rifle shot, and then
> The shrill death-scream of stricken men
> Sank the red axe in woman's brain,
> And childhood's cry arose in vain."

The inscription on the monument on the green in front of the Pocumtuck shows the interest Deerfield takes in its past and present history.

The next town to the north is Greenfield, the shire town of Franklin County, and one of the most enterprising on the route. The streets are wide, pleasantly laid out, and the houses present a neat architectural appearance. The best hotel is the Mansion House, George Doolittle, proprietor. There is a Restaurant, Barber Shop, Billiard Room and Livery, connected with the House.

Passing through Bernardston, South Vernon, Vernon and Fort Dummer, where the first settlement in Vermont was made, and we come to Brattleboro, a description of which was given in our article on the Green Mountains. We are now on the line of the Vermont Central Railroad, and passing through Dummerston, Putney, East Putney, Walpole, Bellows Falls, and the route through Windsor, (also described in our Green Mountain division), we come to White River Junction. Passengers for Mount Mansfield, Burlington, St. Albans and Montreal, keep the Vermont Central. Passengers for the White Mountains and Lake Memphremagog take the Pasumpsic. The Junction House, A. T. & O. F. Barron, proprietors, is pleasantly located at White

POCUMTUCK HOTEL, DEERFIELD, MASS.

CHARLES O. PHILLIPS, Proprietor.

River Junction, and is a desirable house for the business man or tourist. The rooms are large and well furnished, and tables well supplied. A good livery and billiard-tables are connected with the house. Passengers leaving New York by morning trains, or Boston by evening trains, destined for the White Mountains or Lake Memphremagog, often remain over night at the Junction House, proceeding the next morning at eight o'clock.

This is the regular dining-place for all trains on Vermont Central, Passumpsic and Northern Railroads. Ample time is given for all meals, and the departure of all trains announced by the conductors. Passengers leaving Springfield by morning trains, stop here twenty-five minutes before proceeding to the White Mountains or Lake Memphremagog. This has enjoyed for a long time the reputation of being the best Railroad Ea'ing House in the Eastern States. A person has an opportunity of being seated at a table, and *enjoying* a meal, and time is given for something more than a promiscuous disposal of viands.

Leaving White River Junction for the mountains or lake, we pass through Norwich, Pompanoosuc, Thetford, North Thetford, Fairlee, Bradford, South Newbury, Newbury, and come to Wells River, forty miles north of White River Junction, where the White Mountain Railway connects for Littleton, Whitefield, Lancaster and Bethlehem. From Wells River, *en route* for the lake, we pass through Ryegate, McIndoes, Barnet, McLeran, Passumpsic to St. Johnsbury, one of the most flourishing towns in Vermont. Here is located the large Scale Manufactory of the Messrs. Fairbanks.

Passing through St. Johnsbury Centre, we come to Lyndonville, where the offices and machine-shops of the Passumpsic Railway are located. It is a new village and finely laid out.

Passing through West Burke, South Barton, Barton Landing and Coventry, we come to Newport and Lake Memphremagog, a reference to which we have already given. From Newport passengers pursue their northern journey. Making a route from New York to Quebec, seventy miles shorter than by any other line. The whole route is admirably conducted from the Grand Central Depot of New York to the old Dominion Capital on the St. Lawrence.

FOR THE LAWN, THE GARDEN WALK, THE PARLOR AND THE PIAZZA.

GAME OF MAGIC HOOPS.

A COMPANION TO CROQUET.—Every Croquet ground should have MAGIC HOOPS for variety. For sale everywhere with Croquet.

Remember the name; Don't take some other game with a similar name.

Send stamp for Illustrated Catalogue of Home Amusements to **MILTON BRADLEY & Co.**, Springfield, Mass.

NEW YORK TO NEWPORT, BOSTON, PORTLAND AND THE WHITE MOUNTAINS.

The all rail lines from New York to Newport and Boston, are *via* the New York and New Haven Railroad to New Haven, and from New Haven by the Shore Line to Wickford and Newport, and also *via* Providence to Boston. Another route passes from New Haven to Boston, through Hartford, Springfield and Worcester. Of the Sound Lines for Boston or Newport, we are inclined to give preference to the "Stonington Steamboat Co.," as it avoids Point Judith, that *projection* of land and of *victuals* somewhat dreaded by unseaworthy people. The Wickford branch connects with the Stonington steamboats and the Shore Line Railroad. From New York to Portland and Mount Desert, there is a succession of sea side resorts to which we propose in brief to call attention. The principal points on the New York and New Haven Railroad, of which we catch glimpses in our journey are Harlem, eight miles from the City Hall. Harlem River, Morrisania, West Farms, Williams Bridge, Woodlawn Cemetery, Mount Vernon, Pelhamville and New Rochelle, where Thomas Paine died, 1809. His monument still remains here. His remains however were removed to England by Mr. William Cobbett, who visited this country and wrote his biography. Passing through Mamaroneck, an Indian name said to denote the place of rolling stones, Rye with its famous beach, Stamford, with its pleasant residences, Bridgeport with its thriving factories, Stratford, with its quiet streets, and we come to New Haven, the semi-capitol of Connecticut. This is one of the finest cities in our country, and in the very centre is the famous green, occupying about sixteen acres. Temple street passes through it, north and south, and fronting this sylvan way are three churches, Centre, North and Trinity. In the rear of Centre Church stands a monument to the memory of John Dixwell, one of the regicides, for many years secreted in New Haven. West of this, the State House, said to be built after a model of the Pantheon at Rome. It looks well by moonlight. West of the "Green" are a long line of brick buildings, which we believe were *not* constructed after the model of the Pantheon—Yale College, the substantial University of New England, named after Elihu Yale, Governor of the East India Company, who was born at New Haven, and was the principal foreign donor. It was originally founded in Killingworth, 1700; chartered, 1701; removed to Saybrook, 1707; removed to New Haven, 1716.

NEW HAVEN HOUSE.   S. H. MOSELEY.

It has imparted instruction to a greater number of students than any other institution in the United States. The Divinity school and new dormitories are being completed. The Art Building, the finest in the State, was completed, 1867. The Alumni Hall and Library are fine buildings. Every visitor is interested in the college, its traditions and customs,— some of them reaching back to the early times of the colony. The New Haven House, opposite the Green, and diagonally opposite the College-green, is by far the best hotel in the city, and one of the best hotels to be found in this country. Dr. Holland, in Scribner's *Monthly*, says: "We are not at all afraid that the patrons of this House will fail to endorse all our praise or charge us with extravagance when we declare the New Haven House to be a model for luxury, neatness, order, and thorough good management." It is now owned and kept by S. H. Moseley, who was for ten years connected with the famous Massasoit House, Springfield Mass., and for five years one of the partners of the charming Brevoort House, New York. This hotel also affords the best prospective point for studying college peculiarities. In summer evenings students *congregate* on the college fence and sing the old-time college songs, and at such times the windows and balconies of the hotel are well filled, for many of these impromtu serenades to the old elms are quite as fine as a finished Yale concert. It seems to be the idea of the college to build in the shape of a quadrangle, so that the grounds will be entirely inclosed. Many of the buildings are already commenced. There are many places of interest in the vicinity of New Haven. East and West Rocks, each about two miles distant. The Judge's Cave at West Rock is about half a mile from the edge of the cliff. Those who helped to establish the constitutional liberty of England found refuge here, and New Haven citizens carried them food in their concealment. About half a mile from West Rock is "My Farm at Edgewood," the home of Donald G. Mitchell, who, long ago, ceased to be a "Bachelor in Reverie."

On the opposite page we present a cut of the largest carriage manufactor in our country, now owned by William H. Bradley. There are generally three or four hundred carriages constantly on hand, and every one who has an hour to spare in this city and has taste in this direction, ought to look at some of the finest work anywhere on wheels. By all means all who wish to purchase should first pay them a visit. The harbor of New Haven would be a fine affair if it were only deeper. It is good for oysters, but bad for ships. Long Dock is about a mile in length. A sail on the Sound from New York to New Haven, is one of the finest that can be taken to or from any point.

About three miles from New Haven, and connected with it by horse cars, is the Sea View House, recently built near the old site of the Savin Rock. It forms a fine landmark to the steamer coming up the harbor. Trains on the New York and New Haven Rail Road also stop within a mile of the shore. The horse cars run every fifteen minutes

to and from New Haven and Savin Rock. West Haven sea shore is noted for its superior bathing privileges and fine groves, and has long been a great summer resort for pic-nic excursions from the surrounding country. It is a first class house in every particular with fine beach, fine drives, and easy of access. Richard Dyer, Proprietor. During the Revolutionary war the British landed on this shore, marched into New Haven, and burnt part of the city. Returning to New Haven we take the Shore Line Rail Road, and passing through Branford Point we come to the quiet village of Guilford—the home and burial place of Fitz Green Halleck. The town is as quiet as Stratford on Avon, and looks almost as ancient. There is a charm about these old New England towns, and a soothing sense of undisturbed happiness, where the waters ebb and flow even as sleep and toil rise and fall on the beaten beach of life. The depot is situated half-way between the village and Guilford Point. The "Pavilion," J. M. Hunt, Proprietor, is one of the oldest and best known seaside resorts in the country. This is also one of the finest oyster points on the Sound, and this, together with the beauty and fertility of the shore, made it one of the great seaside resorts among the Indians. And it is a singular fact that when they were here buried, oysters were also placed in the grave—an evidence of the custom referred to in Hiawatha:

> "Only give them food to carry,
> Only give them fire to light them,
> Four days is the spirit's journey
> To the land of ghosts and shadows."

The next place of seaside interest is Fenwick Hall, Saybrook, D. A. Rood, Proprietor; also proprietor of the largest hotel in Connecticut, the United States of Hartford. The Connecticut Valley Rail Road leaving Hartford as its northern terminus, passes through Middletown and crosses the Shore Line. Passengers *via* Shore Line connect with the Connecticut Valley at the Junction. Fenwick Hall station is only about forty rods from the house, and tickets are sold and baggage checked from New York, Providence, and Hartford directly to the house. New York passage can also be obtained on the fine steamers of the Hartford and New York Steamboat Company. It is the intention of the proprietor

to make it one of the most comfortable houses of any seaside resort on the coast. The company own two hundred and fifty-one acres of excellent land, on which stands a fine grove of timber bordering on the South Cove. The "South Cove" affords a safe sailing place to children and timid persons, and to "ye hardy mariners" Saybrook Point will always furnish a breeze. The oldest inhabitant (who is still living) hardly ever knew a "dead calm." The drives are exceedingly pleasant. Saybrook is a loyal New England town, as a town should be that has the honor of guarding the mouth of the Connecticut—the great river of central New England.. The fine view of sound, ocean, and landscape is delightful on every side. The hotel faces the sound and presents a front of one hundred and seventy-three feet in length and three stories high, with pavilion towers at either end ; and from the verandah, four hundred feet long and sixteen feet wide, we get a view of the sailing craft and steamers which pass through the sound.

The next town of importance is New London, the southern shipping point of the Northern Transportation Company, making a line from New York to Duluth *via* New London, Brattleboro, St. Albans, Ogdensburgh, and so by Lake to Chicago, Milwaukee, and the Northern Pacific Rail Road.

Two miles from New London is the "Edgcomb House," Eastern Point Groton, Conn., R. S. Edgcomb, proprietor. A large and elegant structure.

The height of the house from base to tower is six stories, and from the top of the tower the eye takes in a vast sweep of the ocean and adjacent islands. In full view at evening, are the government lights at New London, Fisher's Island Sound, Montauk, Gardiner's Island, Plum Island, Bartlett's Reef, Gull Island, &c., and from the broad varandah, which extends on three sides of the house, we have a rich variety of scenery, and the most exhiliarating sea breezes.

There are about thirty acres of land connected with it, and romantic drives and woods adjoining. There is a dock now completed, at which boats plying between Hartford and New London stop, also the steamboat Ella, plying between Watch Hill and Norwich. New York boats

FENWICK HALL, NEW SAYBROOK CONN.

D. A. ROOD, Proprietor.

stop on occasion. A small steamboat runs regularly for the season, connecting with all trains at New London. No finer fishing, boating and sea bathing on the sound. The accommodations of the "Edgcomb," together with the house long known as the Ocean House, and under the same management, are sufficient for two hundred or more guests. The halls are wide and airy, the sleeping rooms are large, each one is well ventilated and lighted with gas, and the arrangements of the entire house have been made with a view to the greatest comfort and convenience of guests. In front of the house is a lawn extending to the beach, affording ample room for croquet and other out door exercises.

STONINGTON

is the next town of importance to the east of New London. This is the eastern terminus of the New York Steamboat Line, and here passengers take the well appointed railway line for Newport and Boston. Passing through Westerly and changing cars at Wickford, we cross the landlocked bay to the great fashionable summer resort of our country.

NEWPORT.

It might be characterized as one of the oldest and newest cities in our country. The modern villa, the tasty cottage and the finished mansion near the sites of venerable buildings, which have a national history and interest.

First among the structures of antiquity on the continent, is the old Tower of Newport, whose origin and builders are shrouded in the deepest mystery. The conjectures in reference to its design and purpose would fill a moderate sized volume. It is circular in form with inside diameter of eighteen feet, walls about three feet thick, and twenty-five feet in height. It is supported upon eight arches, resting upon thick columns, about ten feet high, all built of small pieces of stone firmly put together with mortar. It is now almost covered with ivy, and whatever may be its antiquity, is at least a very unique monument, either to the Northmen of the twelfth century, or a "stone mill" of the seventeenth. Among the other venerable buildings are the ancient State House, the Redwood Library, erected 1748, (among its collection are eighty-four large volumes presented by William the Fourth, King of England), Trinity Church, Commodore Perry's house, the City Hall and harbor fortifications.

The Ocean House, Weavers & Bates proprietors, is the most elegant and fashionable of Sea Side hotels. From the observatory we get a view of all the surrounding country, the first, second and third beaches. The first is used chiefly as a bathing ground by visitors. At the second beach are the well-known Purgatory and Hanging Rocks.

Near to the city is the great Spouting Cave. Every person, whether citizen or foreigner, who wishes to get an idea of fashionable American life, ought to spend at least two weeks at the Ocean House of Newport, and two weeks at Saratoga, the two best representatives of watering places *externally* and *internally* applied. From the Ocean House observatory you can also see Block Island across the "wine colored" deep (without a glass). Newport is also the home of Ida Lewis, the Grace

Darling of our country, and *likewise* the *original* J. A. Williams, who has the photographs, stereoscopic views and pictures of various forms and styles, *taking in* everything of interest in the vicinity of this historic and sea girdled town.

From Newport persons *en route* for Boston take the "Old Colony" Line, *en route* for Saratoga, Lake George and the North *via* Wickford, New London, Palmer and Springfield. Through passengers from New York to Boston will pardon this pleasant divergance at Wickford, and passing through Providence, Attleboro, Mansfield, &c., arrive at the *Capitol* of New England.

BOSTON.

There is so much of interest in and about Boston that we will merely call the attention of travelers and tourists to the various places of interest, and allow them the privilege of being their own commentator. It does one good to find in our rapid age a city progressive and flourshing, *and at the same time*, respecting her own history and preserving her old landmarks. Boston has in truth a worthy pride in her antiquity. To a genuine American the great building of interest on this Continent is Fanueil Hall. From the days of Otis, one of her earliest orators, to the present, it has been the "Cradle of Liberty." The first story it is true, is converted into green grocer stalls and meat markets, but we can pardon an enthusiastic people when we consider that the old Dutch church of New York is used as a Post Office, and the birth-place of Shakespeare, was until quite recently, used as a butcher shop. The Hall above, however, retains its inspiration, and directly over the stage is that fine painting of Webster in his reply to Hayne.

The next place of historic interest is Bunker Hill and its monument. The monument is the great feature of Charlestown, and perhaps, oftener visited than any place in Boston or vicinity. Its height is 220 feet, ascended by a flight of spiral stairs; dedicated in June 1843. It stands however on Breed's Hill, where the battle was fought. Yet Bunker Hill has in name the honor of battle and monument, even as Americus Vespucius defrauded Columbus of his birth-right. Boston Common with its old Elm is also full of history, and somewhat resembles Princes street Garden in Edinburgh. Considering Beacon Hill with its prominent pile of buildings, High street and the State House, the Castle. The walks are well laid out. The old South Church on Washington street with its tall spire is also an ancient landmark. In 1774 the Fathers of the Revolution here met to discuss the affairs of the Colonies. Persons will also find interest in visiting the Custom House, Copps Hill, the Docks, Quincy market, the Boston Public Library (containing nearly 150,000 volumes), Tremont Temple, the Boston Athenæum, Music Hall with its large organ, the new City Hall, and the Statue of Benjamin Franklin with the concise Latin motto, "He snatched the lightning from the clouds and a Republic from tyrants." All who go to Boston will likewise pay Cambridge and "Harvard" a visit, a pleasant ride of two miles by horse car. Near this is the Washington Elm where Washington took command of the American army. The Museum of Professor Agassiz will also detain the visitor, and Mount Auburn Cemetery less than forty minutes ride by horse car from Boston. There are many fine excursions by boat from Boston, Chelsea, Swampscott, Lynn and Nahant, with its famous "Maolis Garden."

The steam Railroad stations are located as follows : The Boston and Maine, on Haymarket square. The Fitchburg, Eastern, and Lowell, on Causeway street. The Providence, at the foot of the Common, on Pleasant street. The Boston and Albany, on Beach street. Old Colony and Newport, Kneeland street. The Boston, Hartford and Erie, at foot of Summer street. The Boston, Clinton and Fitchburg, is on Beach street. The Boston, Taunton and New Bedford station is at the foot of the Common. The Woonsocket branch of the B., H. and Erie R. R. leaves Boston and Albany Depot, Beach street.

Thus in brief we have pointed out some of the principal places of interest. The best hotels are the Revere and the Tremont. To the tourist who is giving Boston a week or a few days visit, the Revere is pleasantly and conveniently located. This has long been the prominent public house in Boston for the best class of travelers or tourists from home or abroad. The Revere fronts on Bowdoin square, and here the horse cars of the Union Railroad arrive and depart for Cambridge, East Cambridge, Harvard square, Watertown, Mount Auburn, Brighton,

&c. It is also the most convenient to the White Mountain and northern travel. It has been remodelled throughout, and its table is unsurpassed. The cut of it is here given, Wetherbee, Chapin & Co., proprietors.

BOSTON TO PORTLAND.

Pursuing our Shore Line route, we take the Eastern Railroad at Boston, on Causeway at foot of Friend street. Soon after leaving the station we cross the Charles and Miller Rivers, and pass through Somerville, one mile from Boston. On the left we see Winter Hill, where Burgoyne and his army were encamped as prisoners of war, *after they had made the round trip to Saratoga.* Charlestown, the City of Bunker Hill Monument, is seen on the right after leaving the Boston Station. Passing through Everett, we come to Chelsea, which, during the last few years has grown rapidly from a town to a city. Population about twenty thousand. Passing through Revere, (once called North Chelsea, but changed in honor of Paul Revere), we came to Oak Grove Station, the nearest station to Chelsea Beach. Passing through West Lynn and Lynn, the great boot and shoe district of our country, we come to Swampscott, 'a famous summer resort, with four beaches on the sea shore. The next town is Salem, sixteen miles from Boston, the principal city of Essex County. This is the junction of the Marblehead Branch. Here is located the car manufactories of the Eastern Railroad. Crossing the track of the Salem and Lowell Railroad and North River, we come to Beverly, another ancient town of Massachusetts. This was the birth place of Nathan Dane. This is also the junction of the Gloucester Branch. Passing through North Beverly, Wenham, Ipswich, Rowley, Knights Crossing, and we come to Newburyport, one of the finest located towns in New England, and the burial place of George Whitefield. Crossing the beautiful Merrimack, whose valley is well known to our country, by the thriving towns of Manchester, Lowell and Lawrence, and also as the birthplace of Webster, and we come to East Salisbury, thirty-eight miles from Boston ; the beach is about two miles from the depot, immortalized by Whittier, in his "Tent on the Beach." It extends from the Merrimack to Hampton River, a distance of five miles. One mile from Salisbury, we cross the line to New Hampshire, and passing through Sea Brook, South Sea Brook and Hampton Falls, we come to Hampton, forty-six miles from Boston and sixty-one from Portland. Coaches leave this station for Boar's Head and Hampton Beach. On the back of the fine stereoscopic views of this famous Beach we find the following concise description—

"BOAR'S HEAD HOTEL, Hampton Beach, N. H.,
S. H. DUMAS, Proprietor.

'Boar's Head is as abrupt eminence ex'ending into the sea, and forming the dividing point between the Grand North and South Beaches at Hampton. On the crown of the promontory this hotel is built. It is so elevated as to command from window and piazza a wide view of the sea, Isles of Shoals, and the Coast from Cape Ann to Portsmouth. The rooms are lighted with gas, well ventilated, and easily accessible. Every convenience has been provided. A telegraph office, post office, billiard hall and bowling alley are connected with the house. It is 10 miles from Exeter, 10 from Newburyport, 12 from Portsmouth, 5 from Rye Beach, and 44 from Boston. Five trains pass each way daily on the Eastern Railroad, making close connections with all adjoining roads. Guests leave the cars at Hampton Station, three miles from Boar's Head, where coaches will be in readiness."

The next Station is North Hampton, where coaches connect with Rye Beach. Passing through Greenland, we come to Portsmouth, the

BOAR'S HEAD HOTEL, HAMPTON BEACH.

only seaport of New Hampshire, and formerly State Capital. The Rockingham House is one of the finest on the coast, and elegantly furnished. G. W. & J. S. Pierce, proprietors. Portsmouth is the best point for reaching the Isles of Shoals, ten miles off the New Hampshire coast. Crossing the Piscataqua River, we find ourselves "Down in Maine," and passing through Kittery, York, Elliott, Brook's Crossing, South

Berwick Junction, Wells, Kennebunk and Biddeford, we come to Saco, the head centre of watering places on the route. The Pool, Ferry Beach and old Orchard Beach. Passing through Oak Hill and Cape Elizabeth, and we come to

PORTLAND.

This beautiful town seated by the sea, as a summer resort has no superior in climate, situated on high and commanding ground, three miles distant from the open ocean, and always favored with a cool and delightful breeze. The views from the eastern and western extremities of the city are magnificent. From the western promenade the White Mountains are distinctly seen, with beautiful sunset views. From the eastern promenade we see "Casco Bay," with its 365 islands, next to the "Bay of Naples" in beauty. Portland is in fact surrounded with charming spots, seaward and landward. A commodious excursion steamer will run daily during the season to Harpswell, a delightful spot, twelve miles east of Portland. The sail passes the islands and gives one a taste of beauty, even on the way to the most famous "clam bake" in our country. There are excellent beaches for sea bathing within short and pleasant drives from Portland. From Portland persons can take the Grand Trunk Railroad for the White Mountains and the Canadas.

For White Mountains stop at Gorham and take stage eight miles to the Glen House, and then eight miles more to the summit of Mount Washington, where persons take the Railway for the Crawford, the Twin Mountain and the Profile. Large and first class steamers run twice a week between Portland and New York; daily between Portland and Boston. Three times a week between Portland and Bangor. Twice a week between Portland and Mount Desert. Three times a week between Portland, Eastport and St. John, and weekly between Portland and Halifax, N. S. These lines of pleasure and business travel make Portland the centre of a large territory, and this together with its beautiful harbor will always make Portland a prominent city on the Atlantic coast. The best hotel is the "Falmouth," being known as one of the finest in New England. It has a frontage on Middle street of 153 feet by 174 on Union, the front is built of Albert stone. The Union side is of brick with iron columns and pilasters. Six stories high on Middle street, and seven on Union. The whole superstructure rests on a granite foundation. Contains 249 rooms, and 10 stairs. Office 30 by 56, and 16 feet high. Dining-room 58 by 72, and 27 high.

The stone was quarried in Dorchester, N. B. Its great height commands a fine view of the city, and magnificent view of the harbor and islands. It overlooks in fact the city and all surroundings. Street cars from Grand Trunk Depot pass the door of the Falmouth.

FALMOUTH Hotel. P. E. WHEELER, PROPRIETOR.

In this sketch of the route from Boston to Portland there has been so much of interest (almost thirty summer resorts besides towns and cities of ancient and modern interest) that we could only, as it were, glance at them in passing, but we have endeavored to make it plain for *coming* generations (and they are all coming this way, at least, once in a life time), that the best route from Boston to the Forest city is *via* the Eastern Railroad, a route always free from dust and heat, and blessed with that which companies can neither purchase nor monopolize—cool breezes from the sea.

HARLEM & HARLEM EXTENSION RAILROAD.

Through Route to the Green Mountains and Montreal.

HARLEM RAILROAD.

I. C. BUCKHOUT, Superintendent.

This Harlem Route is one of the pleasantest for Northern travelers, passing through magnificent scenery, and the thriving villages of White Plains, Mount Kisco, Croton Falls, Brewster's, Pawling, Dover Plains, Amenia, Millerton, Hillsdale and Philmont; connecting at Chatham Four Corners with Western Railroad for Albany, Pittsfield, Hudson, and also with the

HARLEM EXTENSION RAILROAD.

F. C. WHITE, Superintendent.

This route passes North from Chatham, through the delightful Valley of Lebanon, with its fine summer resort, Columbia Hall, and Petersburg Junction, (connecting with Troy and Boston Railroad,) Bennington, North Bennington, Shaftesbury, Arlington, Manchester, the great summer resort at the base of the Equinox Mountain, Dorset, Danby, Wallingford and Clarendon, to Rutland, connecting with trains to Bellows' Falls, Lake George, Saratoga, Burlington, and the North to St. Albans and Montreal.

This Route passes through a delightful country. Take the cars at Grand Central Depot, New York.

ALSO THROUGH ROUTE BY RAIL FROM NEW YORK TO LAKE MAHOPAC.

BARDWELL HOUSE,
RUTLAND, VERMONT.

JOHN W. CRAMTON, Proprietor.

This large and commodious Hotel is located near the Railway Station and in the business center of the town. It has long enjoyed a reputation as a popular place of resort for travelers, as a first-class house in Vermont. The house has recently been thoroughly renovated, and large and pleasant suites of rooms added; a large Billiard-Room opened; and new furniture and carpets introduced. A wing of fifty feet, three stories high, has been added during the last season, to meet the demands of a continual increase in business.

The house is under the direction of a popular and experienced manager, who has been long known to travelers, and will continue in the future as in the past, to meet the wants and merit the patronage of the public. A first-class *livery stable* is attached to the house, where guests can be at all times accommodated at reasonable rates.

Persons desiring to visit the remarkable

SPRINGS AT MIDDLETOWN,

OR THE CELEBRATED

CLARENDON SPRINGS,

will find Rutland a favorable point to stop.

The Drive to both these places from Rutland is Pleasant and Agreeable.

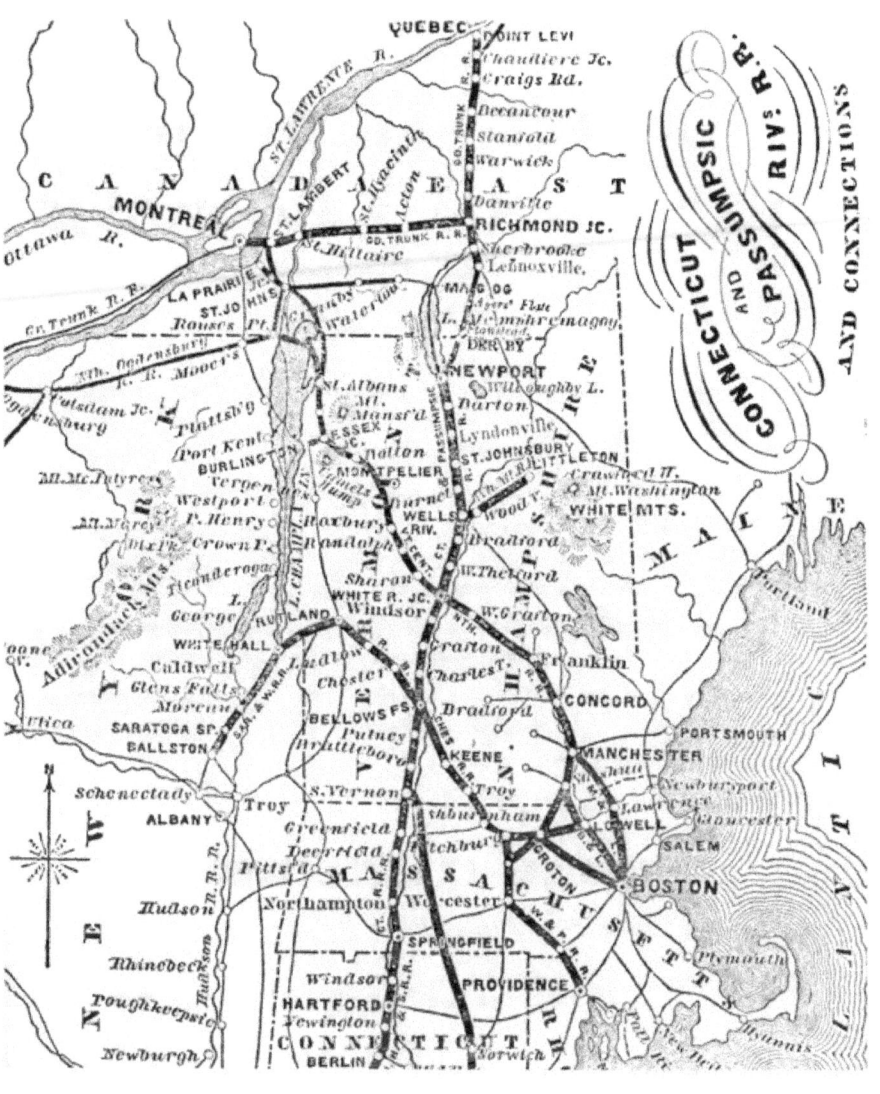

PAVILION,
GUILFORD POINT,

J. M. HUNT, Proprietor.

THIS OLD AND WELL KNOWN

SEA SIDE RESORT

IS PLEASANTLY SITUATED ON

LONG ISLAND SOUND,

15 Miles East from New Haven, one Mile from the fine old town of Guilford, half a Mile from the Shore Line R. R. Depot.

Opens for Company June 20th, Closes Sept. 20th.

Sea-air, Sea-bathing, Sea-food, including Oysters at all times. Boating and Fishing are among its attractions.

All Trains (5 for New York, and 5 for Boston, daily,) stop at this point.

J. M. HUNT.

Guilford, Conn., June 1st, 1872.

PRESENTATION PERAMBULATOR.

PECK & BAKER,

MANUFACTURERS OF

BABY CARRIAGES,

AND

DOMESTIC TOYS.

Factory at Springfield, Mass.   Salesroom 135 William Street, New York.
Illustrated Catalogue furnished on application.
Carriages cased and shipped to all parts of the country.

Newport and Wickford Railroad and Steamboat Co.

RAILROAD ROUTE TO AND FROM NEWPORT, R. I.

This line leaves New York by New Haven Railroad, and passing along the shore of Long Island Sound, through New Haven, New London and Stonington, to Wickford, crosses Narragansett Bay at this point by a ferry of 10 miles, in smooth and land-locked water, reaching Newport in less than 8 hours from New York.

There is no Railroad line in the country which in summer is so cool and free from dust, and this, with the escape it gives from Point Judith, and the discomforts of arriving in Newport in the depths of the night, has already made it as popular as it is attractive.

By this line passengers can leave Saratoga in the morning, and by way of the Boston & Albany and Northern New London Railroads, to New London, and thence to Newport, reach Newport early in the evening; or, leaving Newport at noon, reach Saratoga before 10 P. M.

To those preferring a Steamboat ride to a Railroad, and dreading the rough water and unpleasant results of the voyage around Point Judith, the Stonington Boats leaving Pier 33 N. R. at 5 P. M., are an attractive way of reaching Newport. Passengers going by these boats being landed in Newport early the next morning, after a full night's rest and breakfast on the boat.

STONINGTON LINE FOR BOSTON, PROVIDENCE,
And all parts of NEW ENGLAND.
INSIDE ROUTE AVOIDING POINT JUDITH AND CONSEQUENT SEA-SICKNESS.

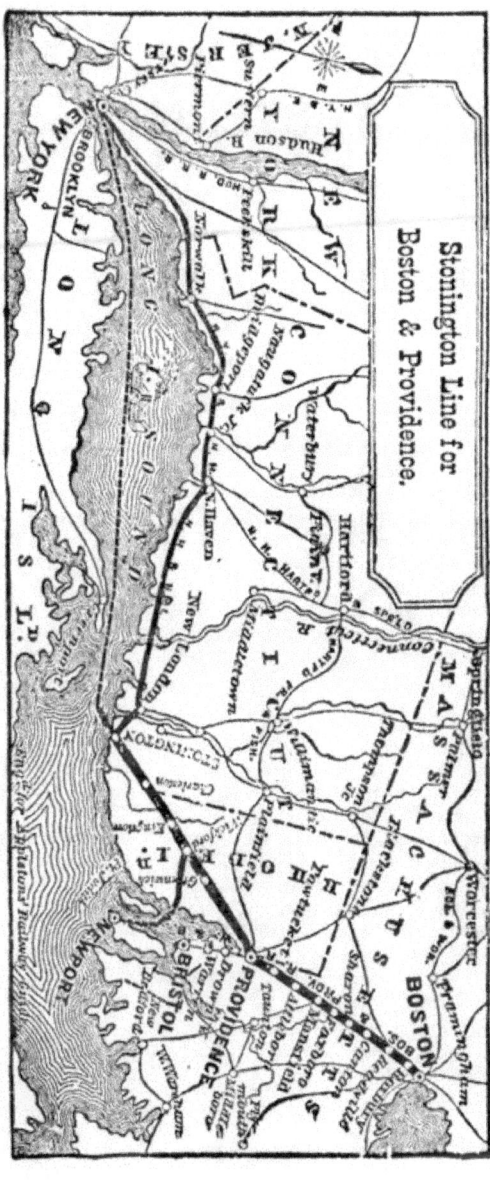

Stonington Line for Boston & Providence.

Elegant Steamers "STONINGTON" and "NARRAGANSETT" leave Pier 33 North River, (near Jersey City Ferry,) alternately, at 5.00 P. M. daily, except Sundays, arriving in Stonington at 2 o'clock A. M. STEAMBOAT EXPRESS TRAIN leaves Stonington at 2.30 A. M., landing passengers in Boston at 6.00 A. M., giving ample time to connect with all trains going East.

Passengers not wishing to take the Steamboat Train, may rest undisturbed until 6.30 A. M., and take the 7.10 A. M. Accommodation Train, arriving at Newport (via Wickford R. R. and Steamboat Co.) at 9.35 A. M., at Providence at 9.00 A. M., and at Boston at 10.45 A. M.

☞ Tickets sold and state rooms secured at No. 319 Broadway cor. New Pearl St., and Westcott Express Offices, New York, and at 82 Washington Street, Boston.

D. S. BABCOCK, President.

NEW ROUTE TO WHITE MOUNTAINS.
1872. EASTERN R.R. 1872.
SEA SHORE ROUTE TO NORTH CONWAY

AND

WHITE MOUNTAINS.

New, shortest, quickest, and only route to North Conway and White Mountains without change of cars.

Two special fast Express trains will be placed on the route on and after June 17th, leaving Boston 8.10 A.M., arriving at North Conway 1 P.M., leaving Boston 2.40 P.M., arriving at North Conway 7.30 P.M.

A fast line of coaches will run in connection with the trains to Crawfords and Glen, leaving North Conway 8 A.M., arriving at Crawfords 1 P.M., leaving North Conway 2 P.M., arriving at Crawfords 6 P.M., leaving North Conway 8 A.M., arriving at Glen 1 P.M., leaving North Conway 2 P.M., arriving at Glen 6 P.M. Distances, North Conway to Crawfords 25 miles, North Conway to Glen 20 miles.

No other route offers so good advantages, 21 miles shorter to North Conway, 62 miles shorter to Crawfords, 50 miles shorter to Glen than *via* any other route.

```
            Fare:—Boston to North Conway  $5.00
                   "      "    Crawfords    8.50
                   "      "    Glen         7.00
```

The only line running the celebrated Pullman Cars between Boston, North Conway and White Mountains.

It is the only line whereby passengers can leave the top of Mount Washington in the morning and arrive in Boston same night.

Time—leave Mount Washington 6 A.M., arrive at Glen (Breakfast) 8 A.M., arrive at North Conway at 1 and 2 P.M., arrive at Boston 7 P.M.

Passenger trains are equipped with all modern improvements, including Westinghouse Air Brake and Miller's Coupler Buffer and Platform.

Be sure and ask for tickets *via* Eastern R.R., the short and favorite route (to be obtained at all the principal Ticket Offices), and enjoy superior accommodation.

Seats in Parlor Car can be secured by letter or telegraph at the Line Office 134 Washington Street, Boston, Mass.

GEORGE F. FIELD, *General Passenger Agent.*

J. PRESCOTT, *Superintendent E. R.R.*

BOSTON, *June* 1, 1872.

EASTERN R.R.

GREAT INTERNATIONAL ROUTE

AND

MAIL LINE.

The Eastern, in connection with the Maine Central and European and North American Railroads, forms the only all rail route from Boston to Portland, Augusta, Bangor, Houlton, Woodstock, St. Stephens, St. Andrews, Calais, St. John, Fredericton, Annapolis, Prince Edward Island, Halifax, and all points in the British Provinces.

It is the only line running a night Express train to Portland, Augusta and Bangor, securing to the passenger a good night's rest, and a saving of twelve hours in time to St. John over any other route.

The only one between Boston and Bangor without change of cars, and only line running the Pullman cars between Boston and Bangor.

The celebrated Pullman cars through to St. John by this route only.

The Eastern Railroad runs five trains each way daily (Sundays excepted) between Boston and Portland, and one additional train Monday, Wednesday and Friday.

Connections at Portland with Maine Central, Grand Trunk, Portland and Ogdensburg, Portland and Rochester Railroad. International Steamship Company for Eastport and St. John, Yarmouth Steamship Company for Yarmouth and St. John, Portland and Halifax Steamship Company for Halifax and Bangor, Machias and Mount Desert Steamship Company.

Passenger trains are equipped with all modern improvements, including the Westinghouse Air Brake and Miller's Coupler Buffer and Platform.

Tickets good until used, and fare as low as by any other route.

Baggage checked through.

Ask for Tickets *via* Eastern Railroad Sea Shore route, which can be obtained at all principal Ticket Offices in the United States and British Provinces.

Boston Office 134 Washington Street.

GEORGE RUSSELL, *General Ticket Agent.* J. PRESCOTT, *Superintendent E. R.R.*
GEORGE F. FIELD, *General Passenger Agent.*

MANSION HOUSE,

GEORGE DOOLITTLE, Proprietor,

GREENFIELD, MASS.

Centrally Located,

WITHIN TWO MINUTES' WALK OF THE DEPOT.

REVERE HOUSE,

H. C. NASH, Proprietor,

BRATTLEBORO, VT.

A Short Distance from Depot.

COR. MAIN & ELLIOTT STREETS.

Eastman Business University.
POUGHKEEPSIE, N. Y., ON-THE-HUDSON.

A Practical School for the Times!

Training Young Men and Boys for a Successful Start in Life—Teaching them How to make a Living and for becoming Active Business Men.

Fifteen years ago Mr. Eastman established the first **Business College** in America, introducing a system of **Practical Training** that has since educated more than **Eighteen Thousand** of the present **prosperous business men** of the country. It is beginning to be understood that a man to succeed, become **eminent**, or a **leader in his business** or **profession** must be **practically educated.**— The good sense that is now pervading the minds of the American people on this subject is evinced by the large patronage this Institution is enjoying from every section of the country.

It is not simply a school for the merchant, but the course of study is so arranged as to be of incalculable advantage to all classes of the community, the **Farmer** as well as the **Merchant**, the **Lawyer** as well as the **Banker.** Its specialty is to prepare **Boys, Young and Middle-aged Men** in the shortest time and at the least expense for the active duties of life, **teach them how to get a living, make money, and become enterprising useful citizens.** It does nothing more and nothing less. How well it has succeeded is best known to its thousands of graduates and patrons, to be found in every town in the land.

There are in this country to-day thousands of parents whose greatest concern is the **prosperity of their sons** that are just starting in active life, and to them especially, is presented the claims of this Institution.

A FEW FACTS

IN REGARD TO

Eastman College.

1st, Its Character. It is a *live, practical, common sense school*—conducted by *able, skillful teachers*, and is endorsed by the *most prominent Educators and Business men* of the country.

2d, Its Location. It is located in the *famous city of Schools and Churches*—the most populous, beautiful and healthful city on the Hudson between New York and Albany.

3d, Its Standing. It is the *oldest, largest patronized and only practical* business training school in the country, and stands to-day the *acknowledged head for imparting a thorough commercial education.*

4th, Course of Study. The course of study is *short, practical, useful and reasonable.* It is *just* what every man *needs and will use*, no matter what his *calling or profession is to be.*

5th, Assisting Graduates. It is the only institution that assists its graduates to situations on completing the course. A large business acquaintance, which extends to almost every village and city in the United States, together with the reputation the College enjoys, enables us to provide situations for all who merit and desire them.

6th, Time of Entering. Applicants are admitted any week day in the year. There is no class system, each student receiving individual instruction. There are no examinations at commencement. Boys past the age of 14 years, young men and men of all ages are admitted.

7th, Terms. Tuition for the *Business Course, time unlimited*, $45 00, with a matriculation fee of $5 00. Board in best private families from $4 00 to $5 00 per week. *The total expense of Tuition, Board and Stationary* for the prescribed course of three months is from $110 to $125. Students selecting cheaper boarding places can complete the course at much less expense. *A deduction from the above is made* when two or more enter from the same place at the same time.

NOTE.—We invite *business men, parents and young men* to make a personal examination of the Institution, its original and pre eminent course of study and plan of operation, confident that it will meet their fullest expectations.

The Illustrated College Journal, giving a history of the Institution, practical course of study, and plan of operation, and the College Directory, giving the names, addresses and business of over 3,000 graduates who owe their present success to the Institution, may be had by addressing the President, H. G. EASTMAN, LL.D., Poughkeepsie, N. Y.

[OVER.]

Eastman Business University, Po'keepsie, N. Y.

Interior View of the Practical Department.

CHESTNUT & FIFTEENTH STREETS,
PHILADELPHIA.

OHN CRUMP, Proprietor.   GEO. FREEMAN, Manag

This admirable Hotel, entirely new in building ar furniture, is on the principal promenade in Philadelphia, and we can recommend it as entirely a first class Hotel.

New York Central
AND
HUDSON RIVER RAIL ROAD.

Nine Express Trains daily from the

Grand Central Depot, New York,

4th Ave & 42nd St.

TWO SPECIAL DRAWING ROOM TRAINS

FOR

SARATOGA AND LAKE GEORGE,

(From New York to Saratoga in less than 6 hours.)

Five Through Trains from New York to

NIAGARA FALLS.

The best managed Rail Road in the country.
The most complete in all its appointments.

ALWAYS ON TIME.

Wagner's elegantly furnished Drawing Room Cars run on all through trains.
Sleeping Cars of the line unsurpassed.
The best Route from New York to the West.

J. M. TOUCEY, Supt.   **C. H. KENDRICK**, Genl. Ticket Agt.

CREAM-NECTAR.

Carbonic Acid Gas, when taken into the stomach, produces an invigorating effect upon the entire secreting function—and if prepared in such manner as to be free from metalic substances, becomes a most healthy and delightful addition to all cool and refreshing beverages.

Seltzer, Spa and Pyrmont waters, Champagne, Cider, Porter, and all fermented liquors which are brisk or sparkling owe these properties to its presence—but in all these the Gas readily escapes, and the drink becomes insipid.

If, however, Albumen or Gelatine be added to the solution in which the Carbonic Acid Gas is to be used, a capsule is formed around the bubble preventing its escape, and the beverage then conveys to the stomach the entire quantity.

This combination has been prepared by Dr. WELSH in his **Nectar Syrup**, which, when used with Bi-Carbonate of Soda, makes the most delightful beverage we have ever tried.

The Syrup is put up in convenient pint bottles, and is accompanied with Soda ready for use. Each bottle of Syrup is sufficient for 10 to 12 goblets of Cream-Nectar.

To order address,

Dr. I. L. WELSH,
Jersey City,

P.O. Box 79.   N. J.

CATSKILL LINE STEAMERS,

From Pier 35,

FOOT OF FRANKLIN ST.

Cold Spring, Hyde Park, Staatsburg, Rhinebeck, Tivoli, Malden, Smith's Dock and Germantown.

Passage, ONE DOLLAR.

THE PALATIAL STEAMER

NEVERSINK,

DONAHUE, Commander,

Will leave Franklin St., Mondays, Wednesdays & Fridays,

AT 6 O'CLOCK, P. M.

Making the usual landings.

THE PALACE STEAMER

ANDREW HARDER,

KNICKERBACKER, Commander,

Will leave Franklin St., Tuesdays, Thursdays & Saturdays.

AT 5 O'CLOCK, P. M.

Making the usual landings.

Arriving at Catskill at 5 A.M., connecting with all lines of Stages.

Returning leave Catskill at 6 P. M. on alternate days.

This Line connects with Steamer City of Hudson for Coxsackie, Stuyvesant, New Baltimore, and Castleton.

Citizens' Steamboat Co.

OF

TROY.

THE STEAMERS
Sunnyside and Thos. Powell

WILL LEAVE

NEW YORK, Daily, (Saturdays excpt'd) at 6 o'cl'k, P.M.

From Pier 36, North Moore Street.

RETURNING, WILL LEAVE

TROY, from foot Broadway, Daily, (Saturdays excpt'd)

At 6 o'clock, P. M.

☞ Passengers ticketed and baggage checked via R. & S. and T. & B. Rail Roads to points North and West.

☞ Shippers will mark their freight via "Citizens' Steamboat Co."

G. W. HORTON, Agent, Troy.   JOSEPH CORNELL, Gen'l Sup't, N.Y.

1872  **1872**

NORTH RIVER & NEW YORK
STEAMBOAT COMPANY.

LANDING AT

152d Street,	Dobbs' Ferry,	Rockland Lake,
Englewood,	Tarrytown,	Haverstraw,
Yonkers,	Nyack,	Grassy Point,
Hastings,	Sing Sing,	Verplanks' Point.

PEEKSKILL.

FROM HARISON ST. PIER, Sundays Excepted,

EVERY AFTERNOON

THE STEAMERS	LEAVE AT
CHRYSTENAH,	3.45 P. M.
ADELPHI,	4.00 P. M.
ALEXIS,	5.00 P. M.

CHRYSTENAH. Capt. PURDY.		ADELPHI. Capt. VAN WART.		ALEXIS. Capt. DEAN.	
LEAVE	A. M.	LEAVE	A. M.	LEAVE	A. M.
Peekskill	6.30	Haverstraw	6.20	Nyack	6.15
Verplancks	6.40	Sing Sing	7.00	Irvington	6.35
Grassy Point	6.45	Nyack	6.50	Dobbs Ferry	6.50
Haverstraw	7.10	Tarrytown	7.20	Hastings	7.00
Rockland Lake	7.30	Dobbs Ferry	7.45	Yonkers	7.30
Nyack	8.00	Hastings	8.00	Englewood	7.50
Tarrytown	8.00	Yonkers	8.15	152d Street	8.05
Irvington	8.20	Englewood	8.35		
Yonkers	9.00				

Leaves New York foot Harrison St., 3.45 P.M. for the above landings.

Leaves New York foot Harrison St., 4.00 P.M. for the above landings.

Leaves New York foot Harrison St., 5.00 P.M. for the above landings.

Nyack and Tarrytown Ferry runs in connection with H. R. R. R. trains.

Excursion Tickets and Tickets in packages of 25, at Reduced Rates.

HENRY C. HASKELL,
ALBANY IRON AND MACHINE WORKS,

Nos. 50, 52, 54, and 56 Liberty and 8 Pruyn Sts.

Office, 8 Pruyn Street, near Steamboat Landing,

ALBANY,........NEW YORK.

Successor to Pruyn & Lansing, in this branch of business,

MANUFACTURER OF ALL SIZES OF

STEAM ENGINES AND BOILERS,

BRIDGE AND ROOF BOLTS,
CEMETERY, AREA, AND STOOP RAILINGS;

Bank Counter, Office, and Desk Railings;

IRON WORK OF ALL KINDS.

**Balconies, Verandas, Iron Bridges,
Bedsteads, Bank Vaults, Wrought-Iron Beams,
Roof Crestings, Doors and Shutters.**

MANUFACTURER, ALSO, OF

REZNER, STONE & CO'S
Patent Improved Wrought-Iron Tubular Arch Truss Bridge.

A Lithograph, giving full details, will be sent on application.

Particular attention given to Repairing all kinds of Machinery and Boilers.

Patterns and Models made at short notice.

Send for Illustrated Catalogue.

M'KNIGHT'S UNRIVALED MALT WINE,
BOTTLED AND IN WOOD.
JOHN McKNIGHT'S SON,

BREWER.
Cor. Canal, Hawk, and Orange Streets, Albany, N. Y.
SUPERIOR ALBANY PALE, BROWN, AMBER ALES,
XX AND PORTER.

Analytical Laboratory,
ALBANY MEDICAL COLLEGE, May 2d, 1859.

I have made careful chemical examinations of several samples from different brewings of the article known as "McKNIGHT'S MALT WINE," and find it to be, as represented, a liquid containing nothing but the fermented extract of malt and hops. The different specimens were found to be nearly uniform in composition—the slight difference observed being principally in the amount of alcohol present, owing probably to the varying length of time that had elapsed since the brewings were made.

The Malt Wine examined contained no excess of saccharine matters, such as sugar or honey (as is often the case with similar articles), and which have the effect to mask, to a more or less considerable extent, the peculiar flavor of the hop, and at the same time to diminish the medicinal value of the malt liquors in which they are found. The amount of alcohol contained in the "MALT WINE" is considerably greater than is generally found in American Ales. From the examinations I have made, I am satisfied that the "Malt Wine" is made from carefully selected barley and hops, and is skillfully brewed; that in point of purity, and all desirable qualities, it is fully equal to the best imported ales. As such I can confidently recommend it to the public as an agreeable beverage, and to Physicians as a desirable article for medicinal use. CHARLES H. PORTER, M. D.,
Professor of Chemistry and Pharmacy in the Albany Medical College, Chemist to the New York State Agricultural Society.

FOR SALE EVERYWHERE.
Agencies in all the Principal Cities of the Union.

NORTH AMERICA

(MUTUAL)

LIFE INSURANCE COMPANY,

17 and 19 Warren Street, NEW YORK.

N. D. MORGAN, President.

Assets, - - - - - - $5,750,000.
Deposited with the State, - - 1,693,300.
Income (over) - - - - - 2,000,000.

ABSOLUTE SECURITY.

See what the North America offers—It will be time well spent.

1st. REGISTRY.—This Company issues New York State Registered Policies secured by pledge of Public Stocks, like the circulation of National Banks.

This makes every Registered Policy as secure to the holder as a National Bank Note or United States Bond.

Superintendent BARNES says, in his Report for 1869:—"So far as the question of security is concerned, a Policy duly Registered in this Department, is probably the safest Life Insurance Policy that can be issued by a corporation."

Amount (February 5th, 1872,) on deposit with the Insurance Department, for the protection of the Policy-Holders of the North America Life Insurance Company, $1,693,300.00.

See Regular Bulletin of Registered Policy Account in every Tuesday's *New York Tribune*.
ALL POLICIES REGISTERED IN THE INSURANCE DEPARTMENT FREE OF COST.

2nd. MUTUALITY.—The Company is PURELY MUTUAL, the Capital Stock having been recently paid back to the Stockholders, and henceforth all the profits will be divided among the Policy-Holders, after the NEW PLAN OF CONTRIBUTION originated by this Company.

3d. NON-FORFEITURE.—ALL OUR LIFE AND ENDOWMENT POLICIES ARE NON-FORFEITABLE, thus securing to your heirs the value of every dollar invested, whether you can continue your Policy or not.

4th. NON-RESTRICTION.—No restriction on Travel in the United States or any part of North America, north of the Southern Cape of Florida, or in Europe at any season of the year.

5th. GRACE IN PAYMENT OF PREMIUMS.—Thirty days' grace allowed on any renewal payment and the Policy held good.

6th. PREMIUMS AND RETURNS OF SURPLUS, payable in Cash, or the latter at the desire of the Policy-Holder, converted to additional Insurance.

American Literary Bureau,

NEW YORK, BOSTON and CHICAGO.

ORGANIZED 1866.   CAPITAL $50,000.

JAMES R. MEDBERY, President.   C. S. CARTER, Secretary.

C. M. BRELSFORD, Vice-President.

LECTURE ASSOCIATIONS

Throughout the United States and Canada will find the finest list of Lectures for the coming season in the *American Literary Magazine*, published by the American Literary Bureau.

This Bureau is now prepared to make arrangements for the best talent in the country, among whom we mention the following:

- JAMES ANTHONY FROUDE,
- EDMUND YATES,
- WENDELL PHILLIPS,
- WALLACE BRUCE,
- J. G. HOLLAND,
- ROBERT COLLYER,
- J. E. MURDOCH,
- JOHN G. SAXE,
- MRS. SCOTT SIDDONS,
- BENSON J. LOSSING,
- E. H. CHAPIN,
- HOMER B. SPRAGUE.

For Circulars, Magazine, Applications, &c., address

CHIEF OFFICE,

American Literary Bureau,

Cooper Institute, New York City.

www.ingramcontent.com/pod-product-compliance
Lightning Source LLC
Chambersburg PA
CBHW031453160426
43195CB00010BB/960